Merfolk

a coloring book

Timothy R. Cook

Merfolk: a coloring book

Copyright © 2017 Timothy R. Cook

http://www.etsy.com/shop/TimCookArt

ISBN: 1547101261
ISBN-13: 978-1547101269

Printed by CreateSpace, an Amazon.com company.

Cover and interior illustrations by Timothy R. Cook.

Preface

This coloring book, a continuation of the previous volume, 'Mermaids', is a compilation of forty-eight drawings divided into four sections.

Acknowledgments & Inspiration

Alphonse Mucha's art is the primary source of inspiration for the technical style and fashion design of these drawings, and the graceful elegance and inherent strength of ballet with its fluid lines of form and motion are the most important stylistic influence. Underwater photographers like Howard Schatz, Zena Holloway, Vitaly Sokol, Todd Essick, Shawn Heinricks, and others have all been instrumental in the development of the vision surrounding these mermaids.

Part I

Colors by _____

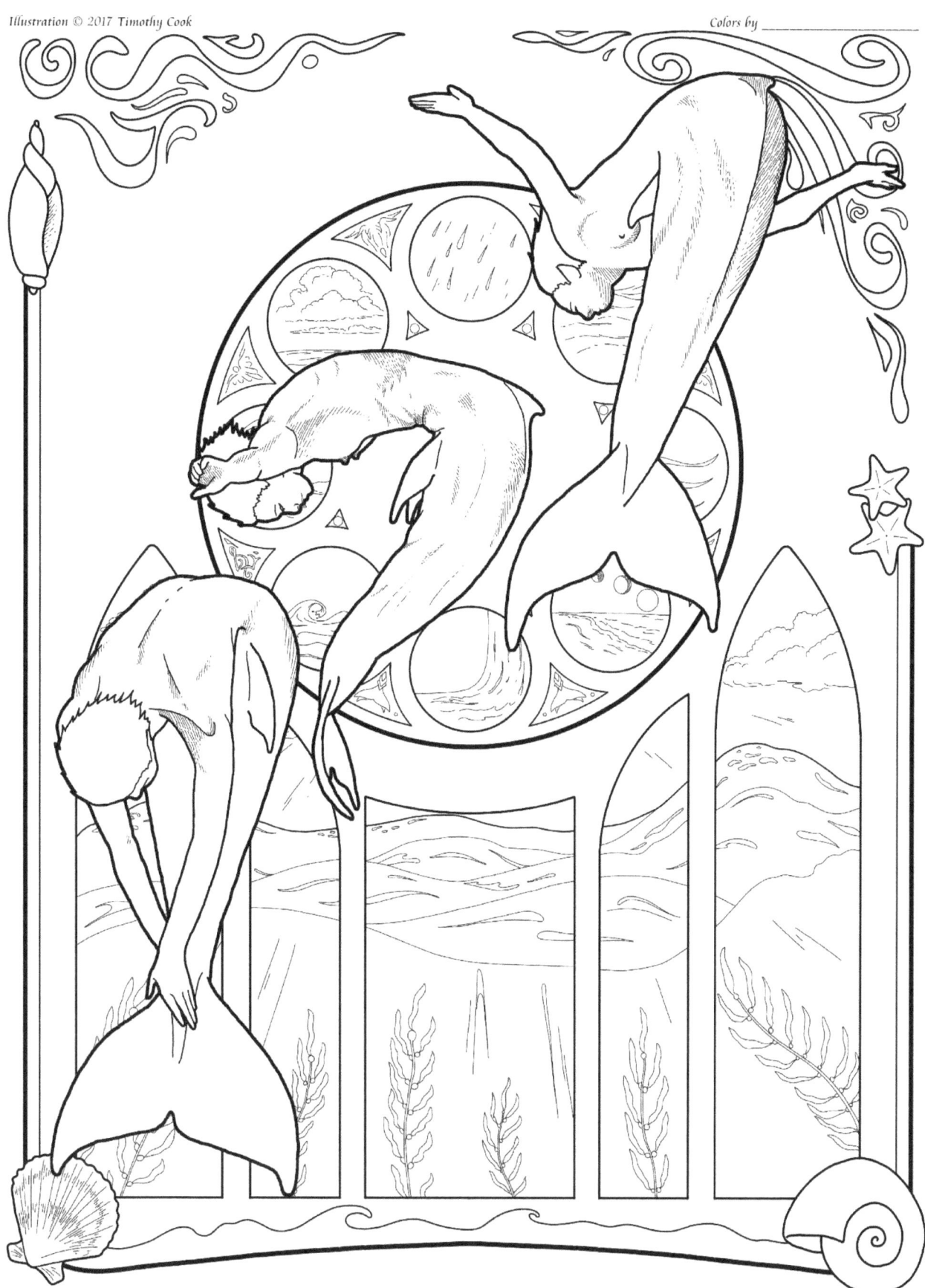

Colors by _____

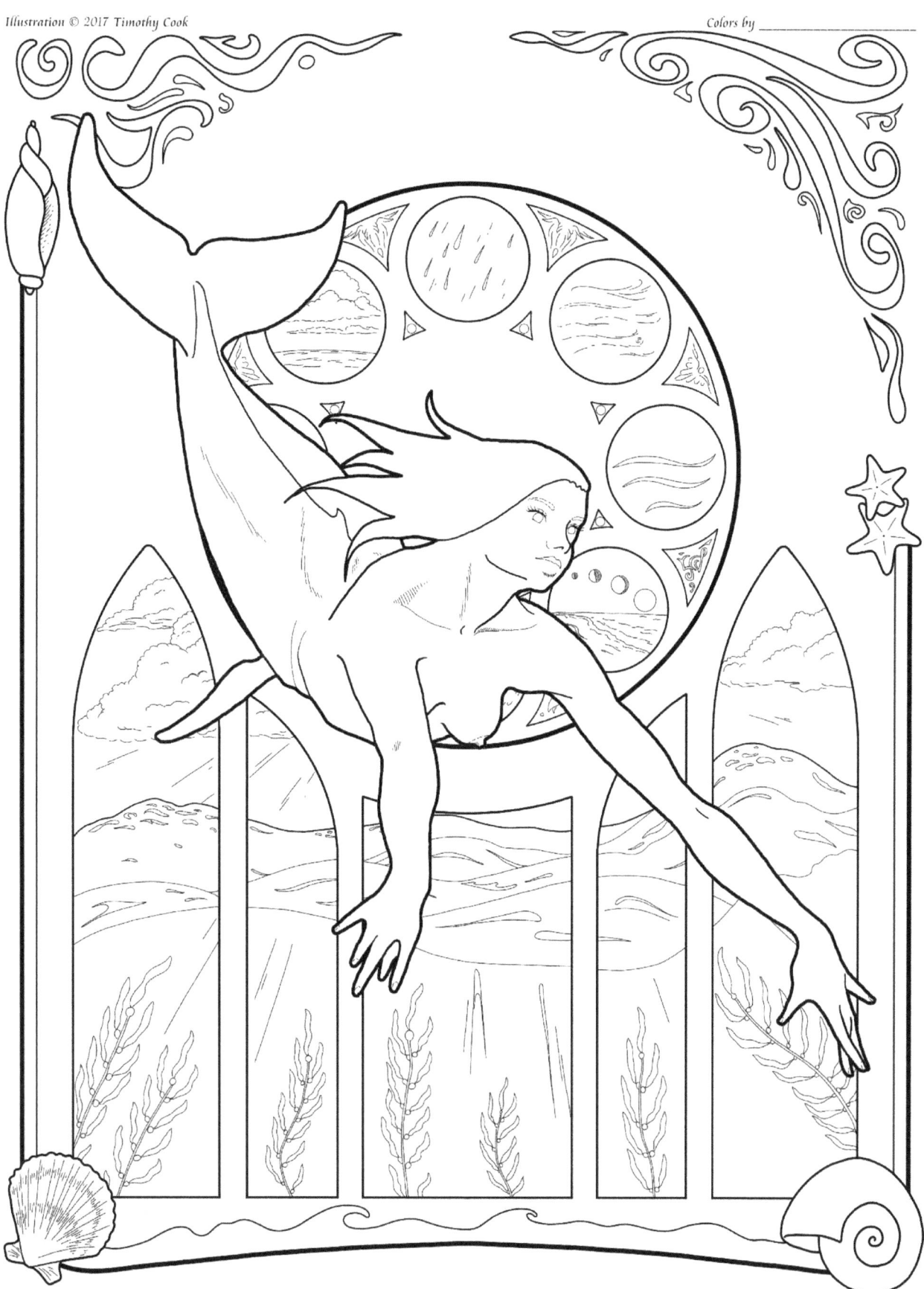

Colors by _____

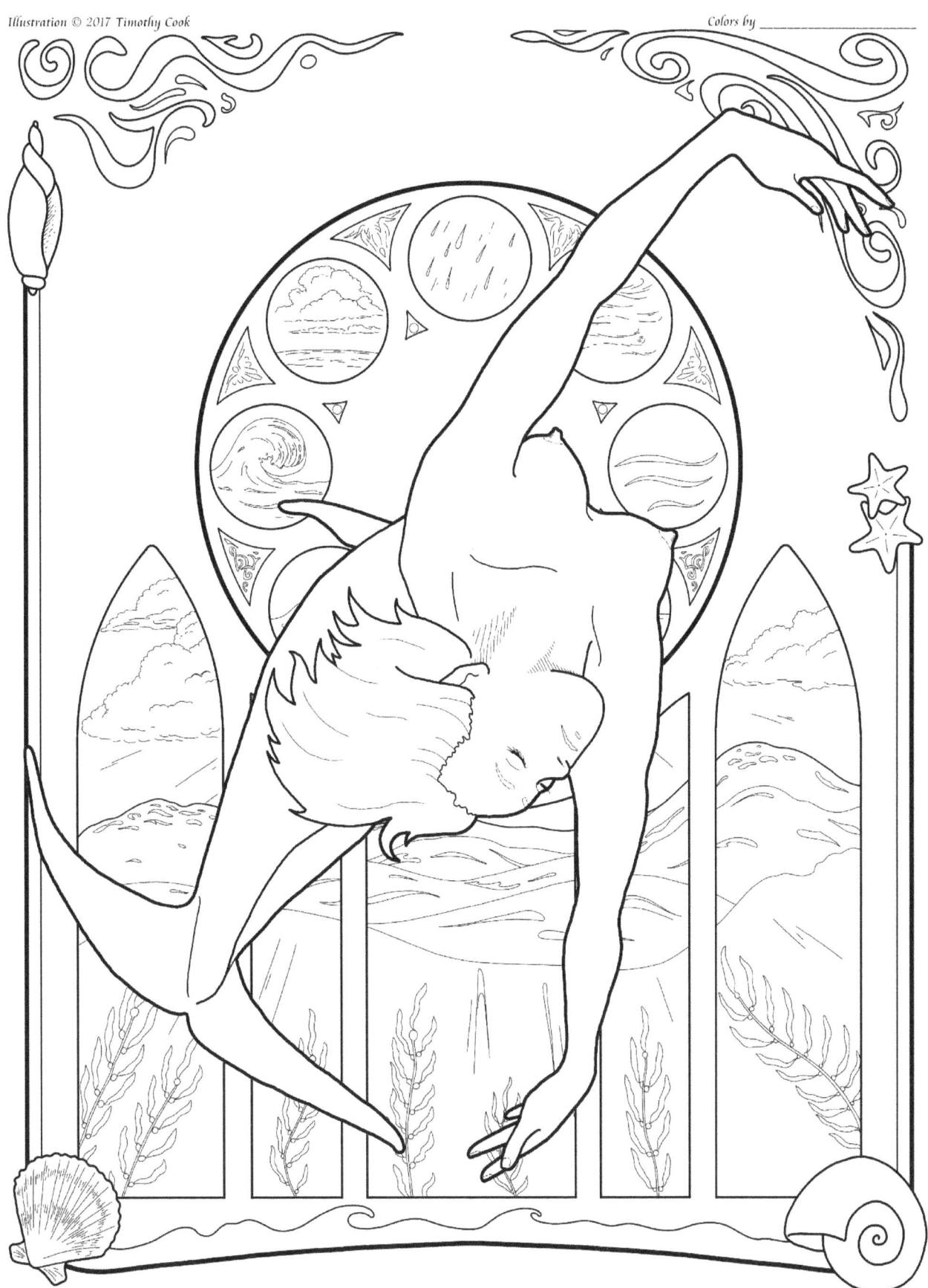

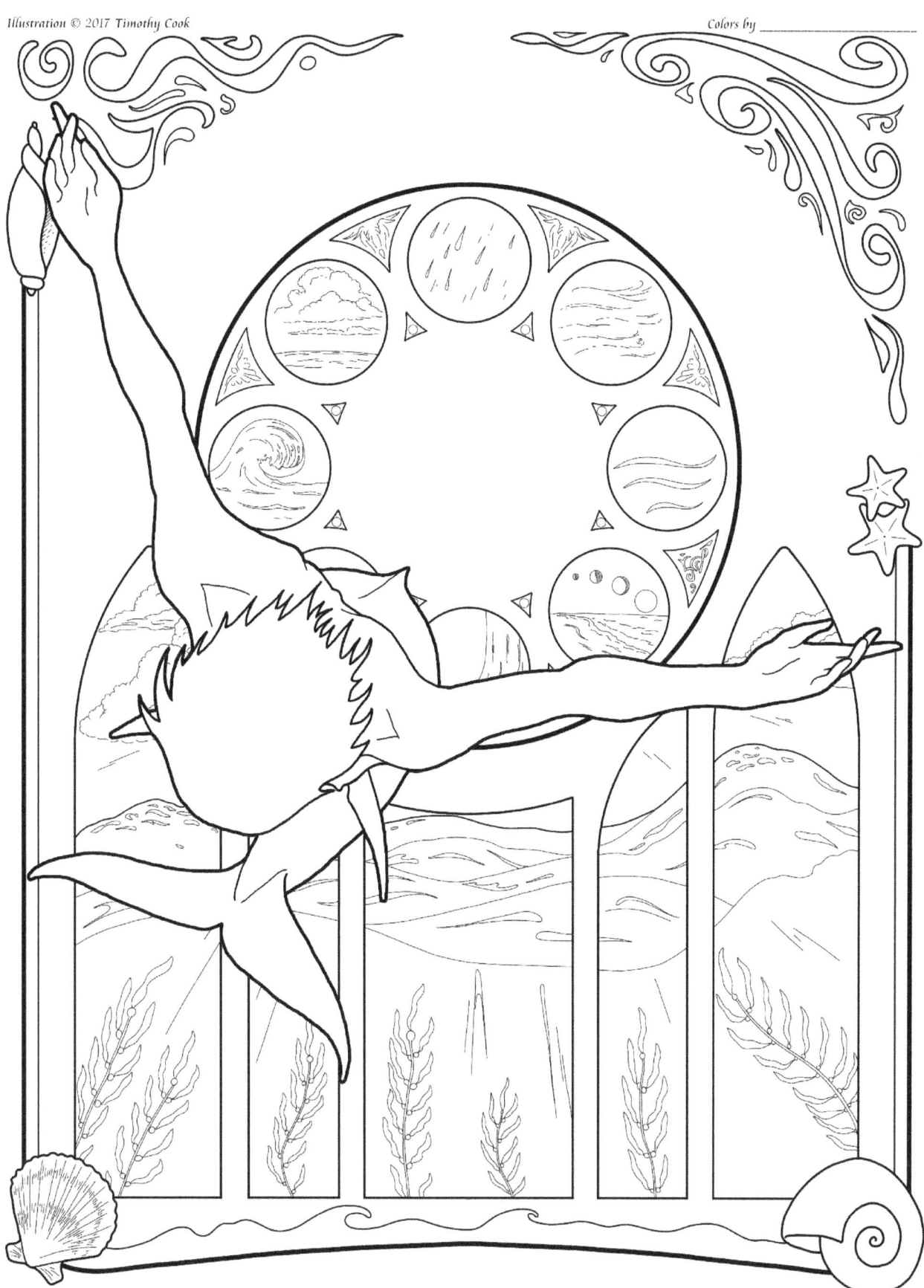

Colors by _____

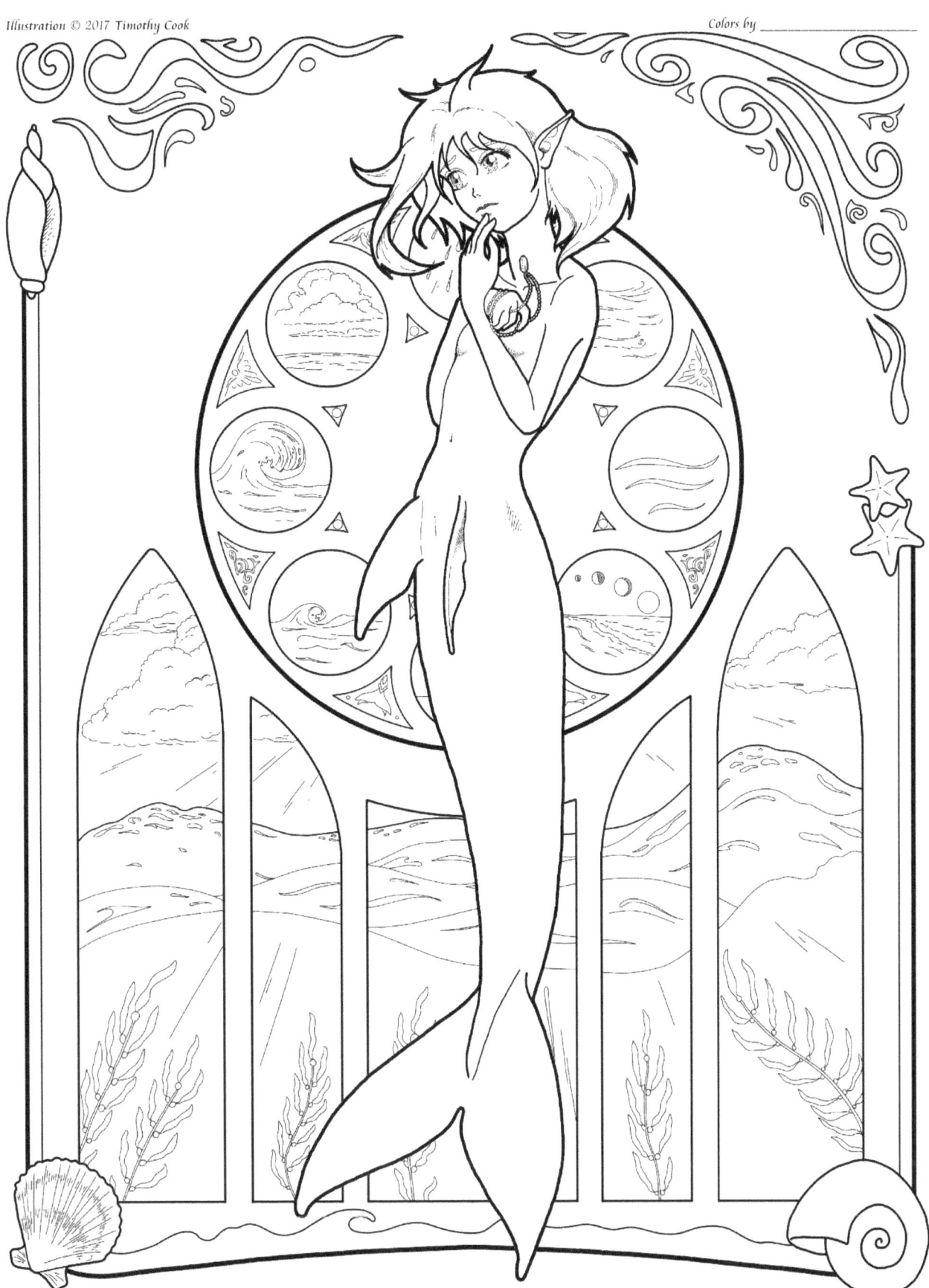

Colors by _____

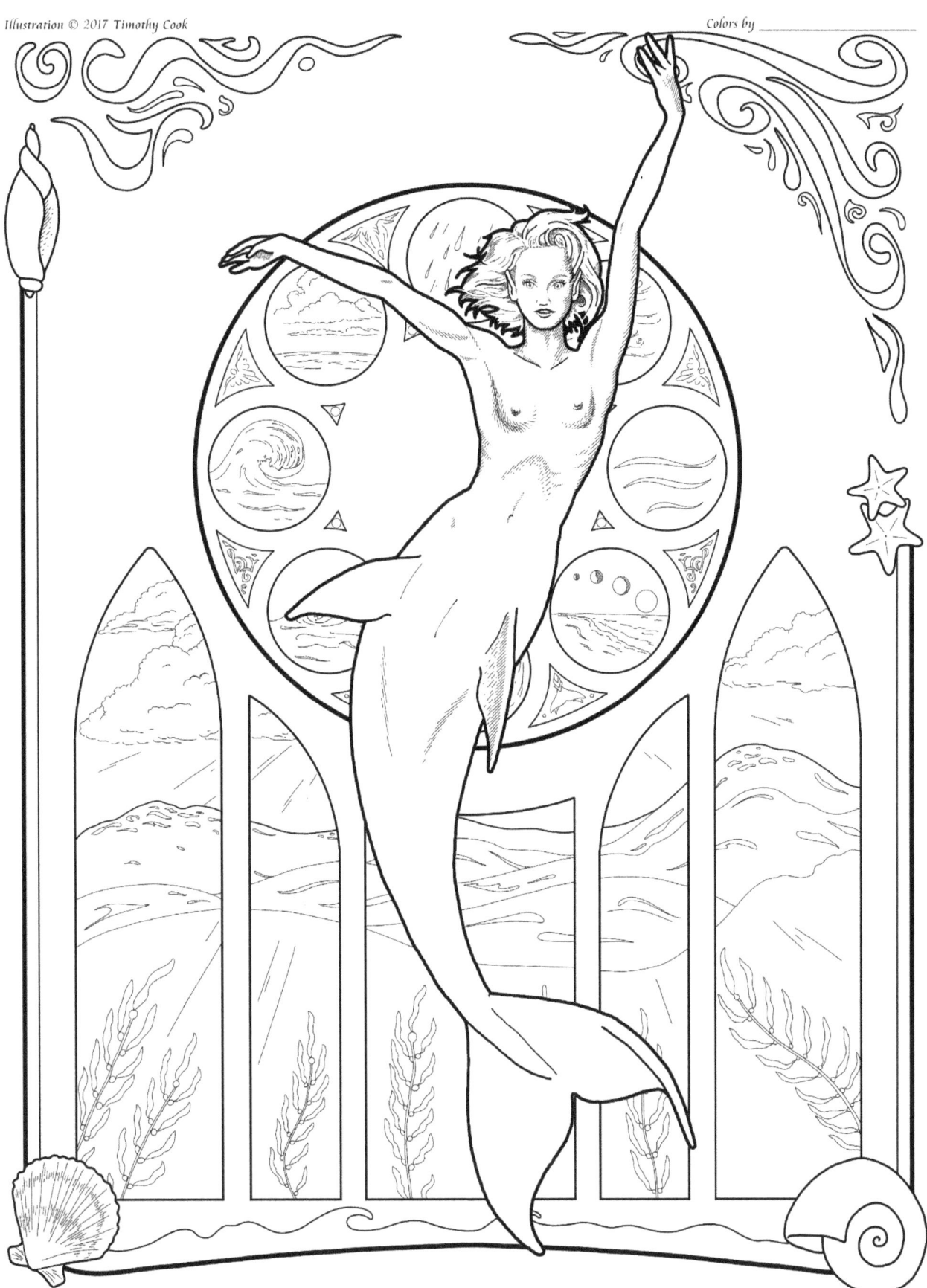

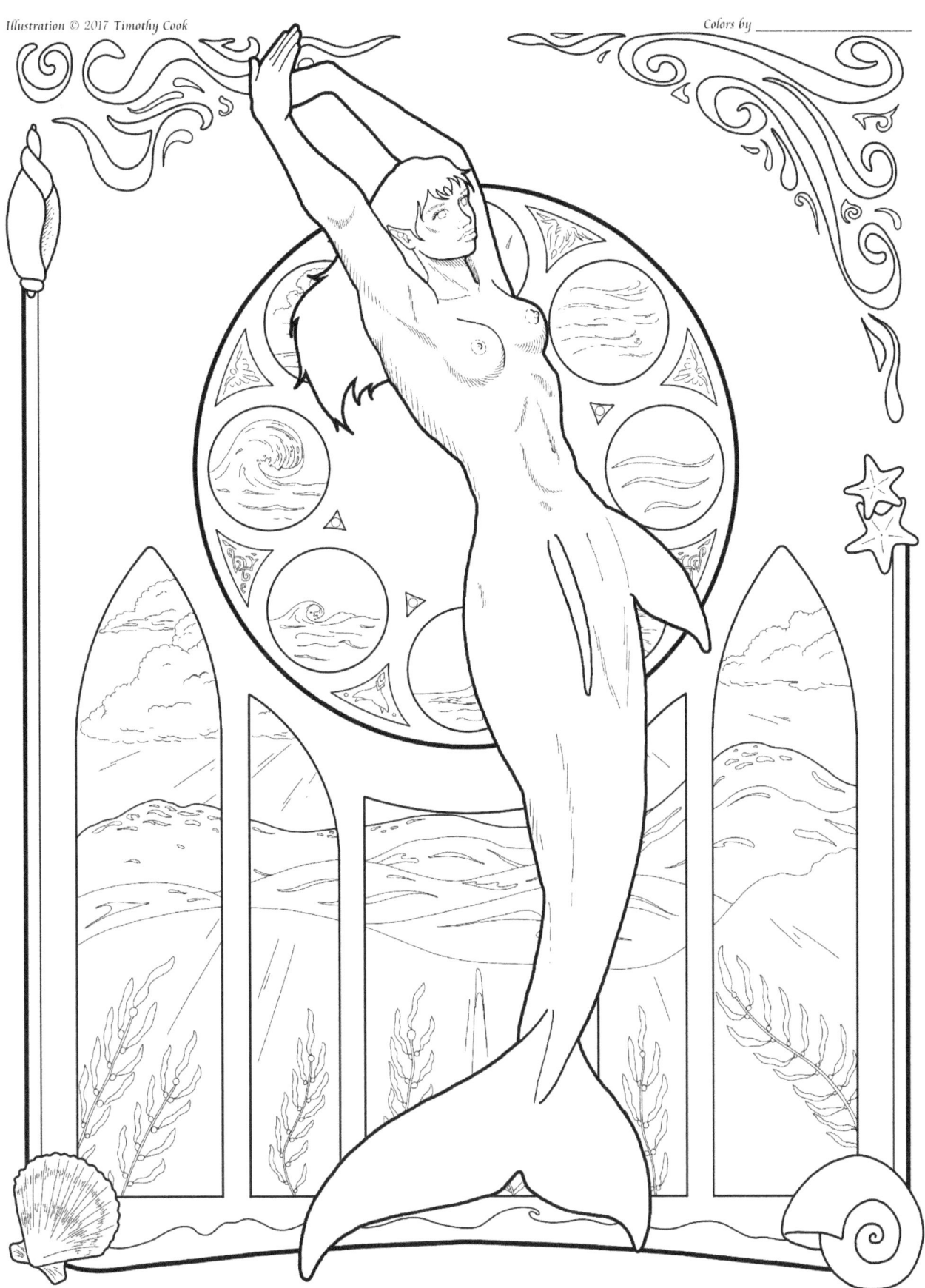

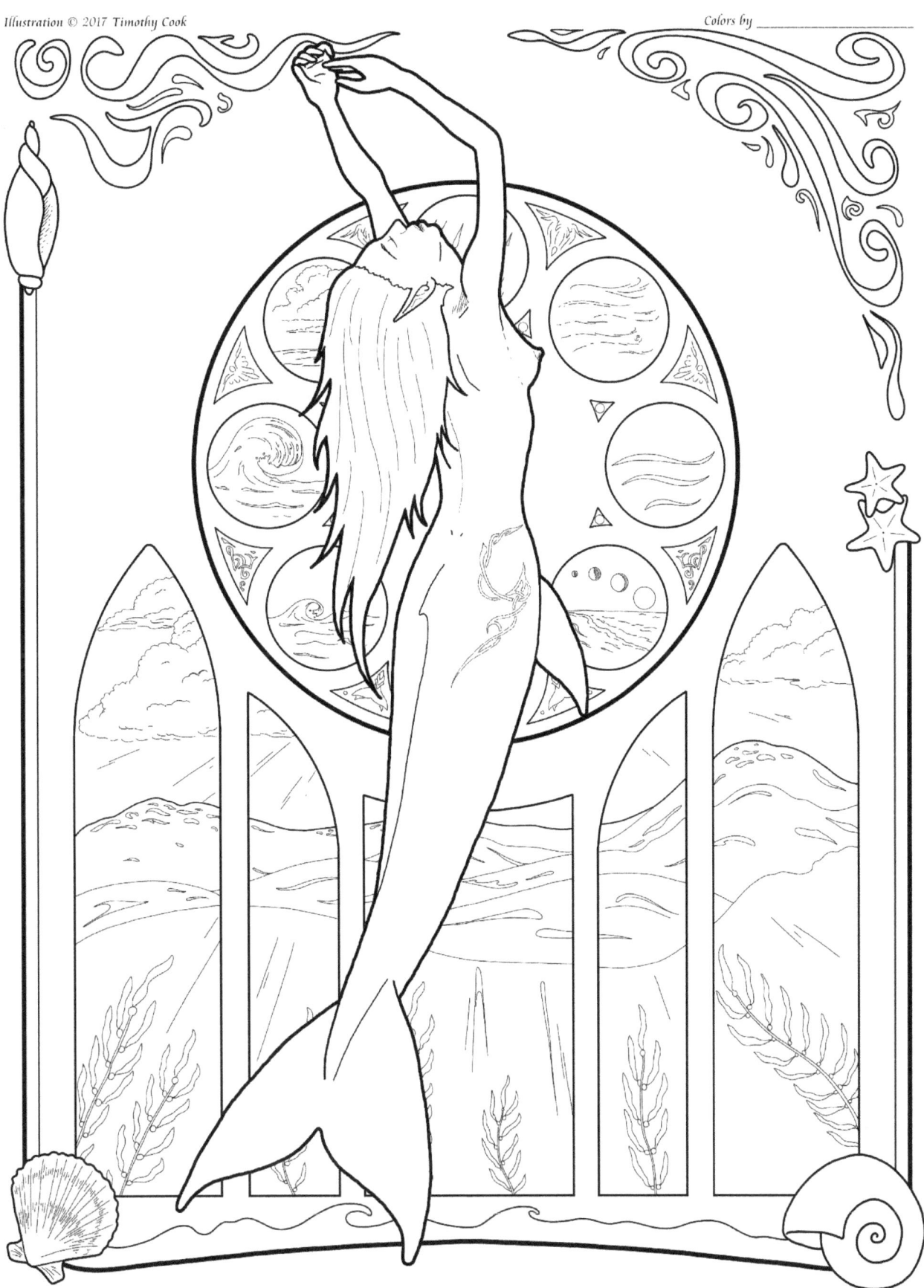

Colors by _____

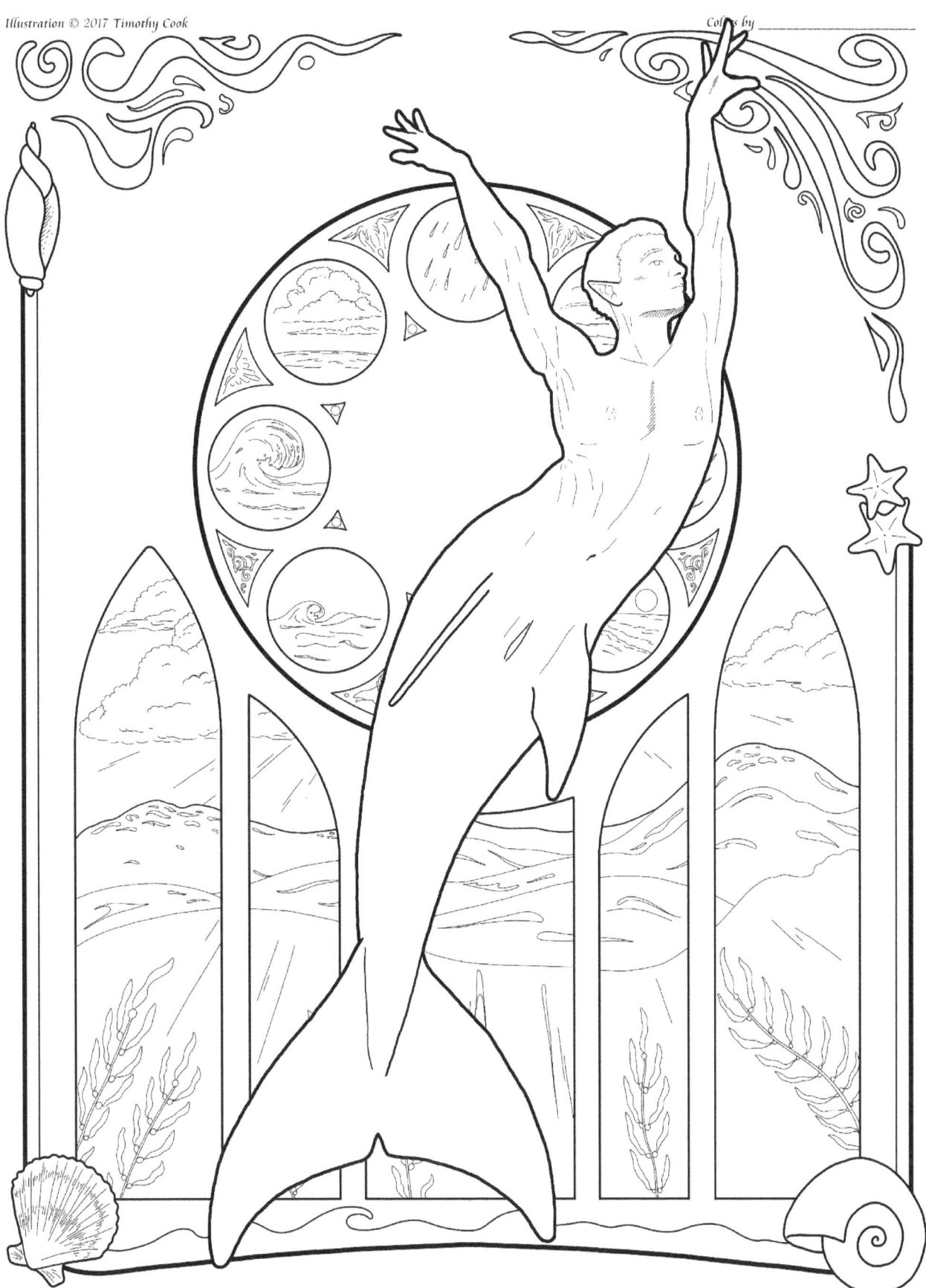

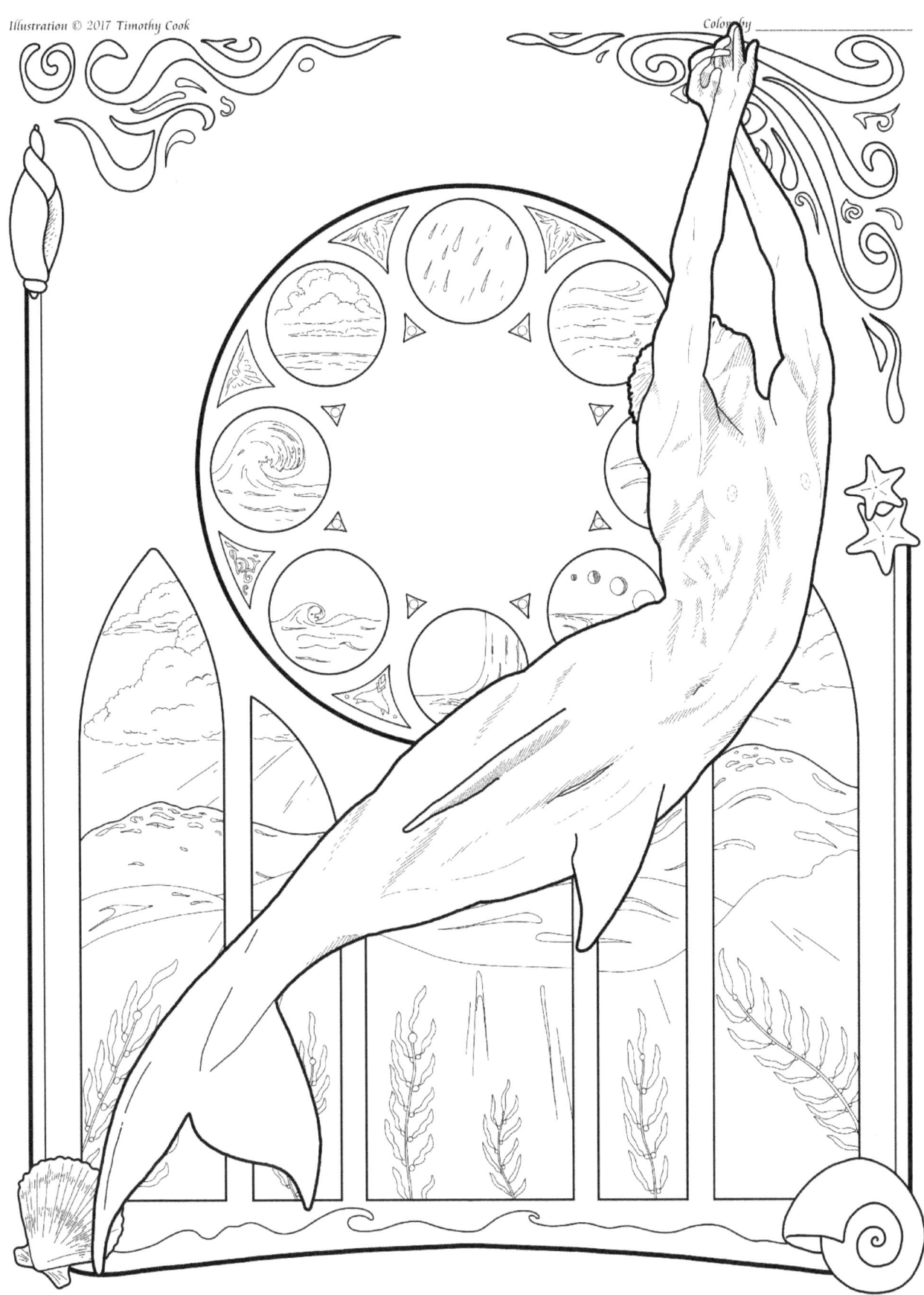

Illustration © 2017 Timothy Cook

Color by _____

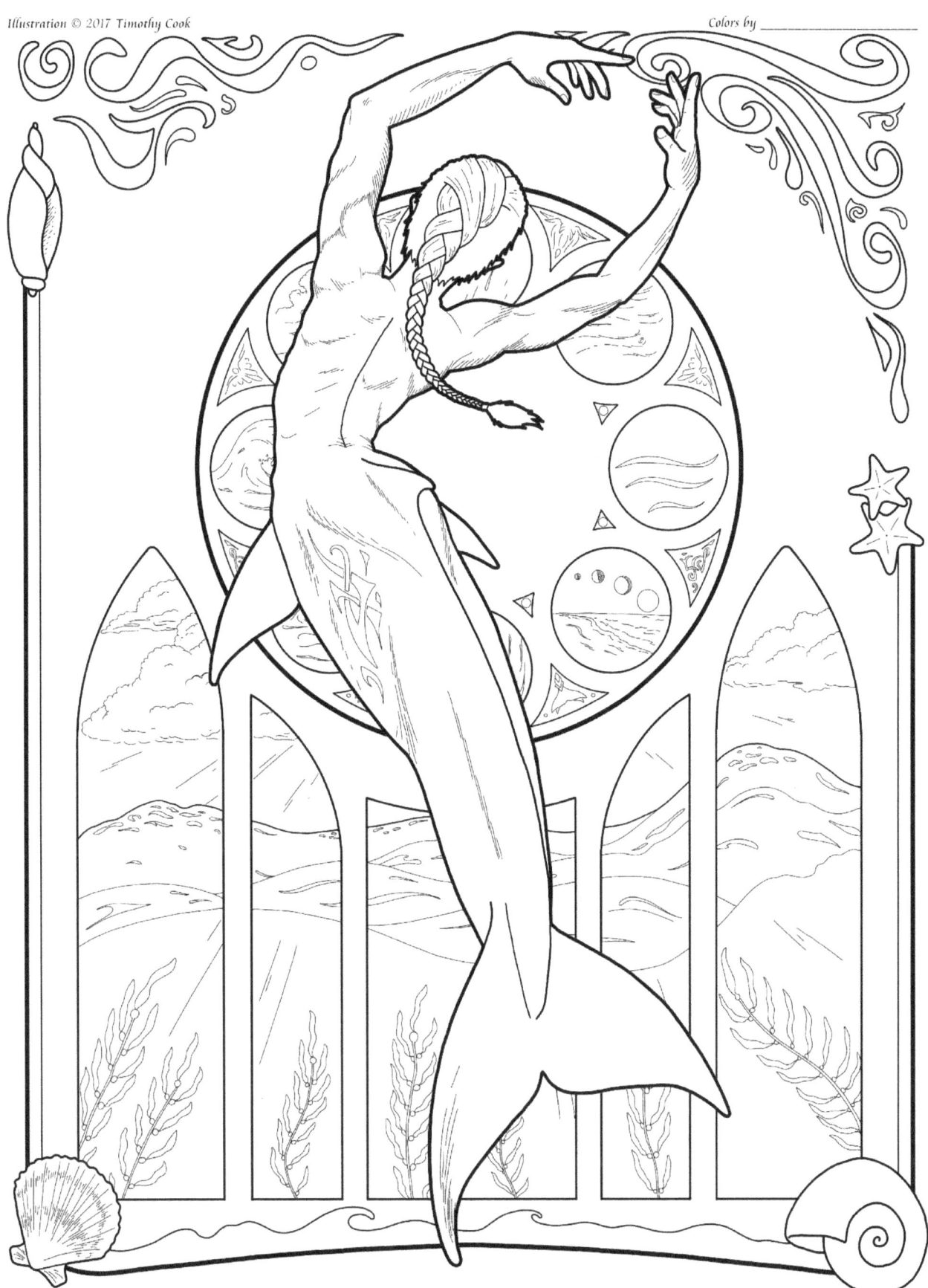

Colors by _____

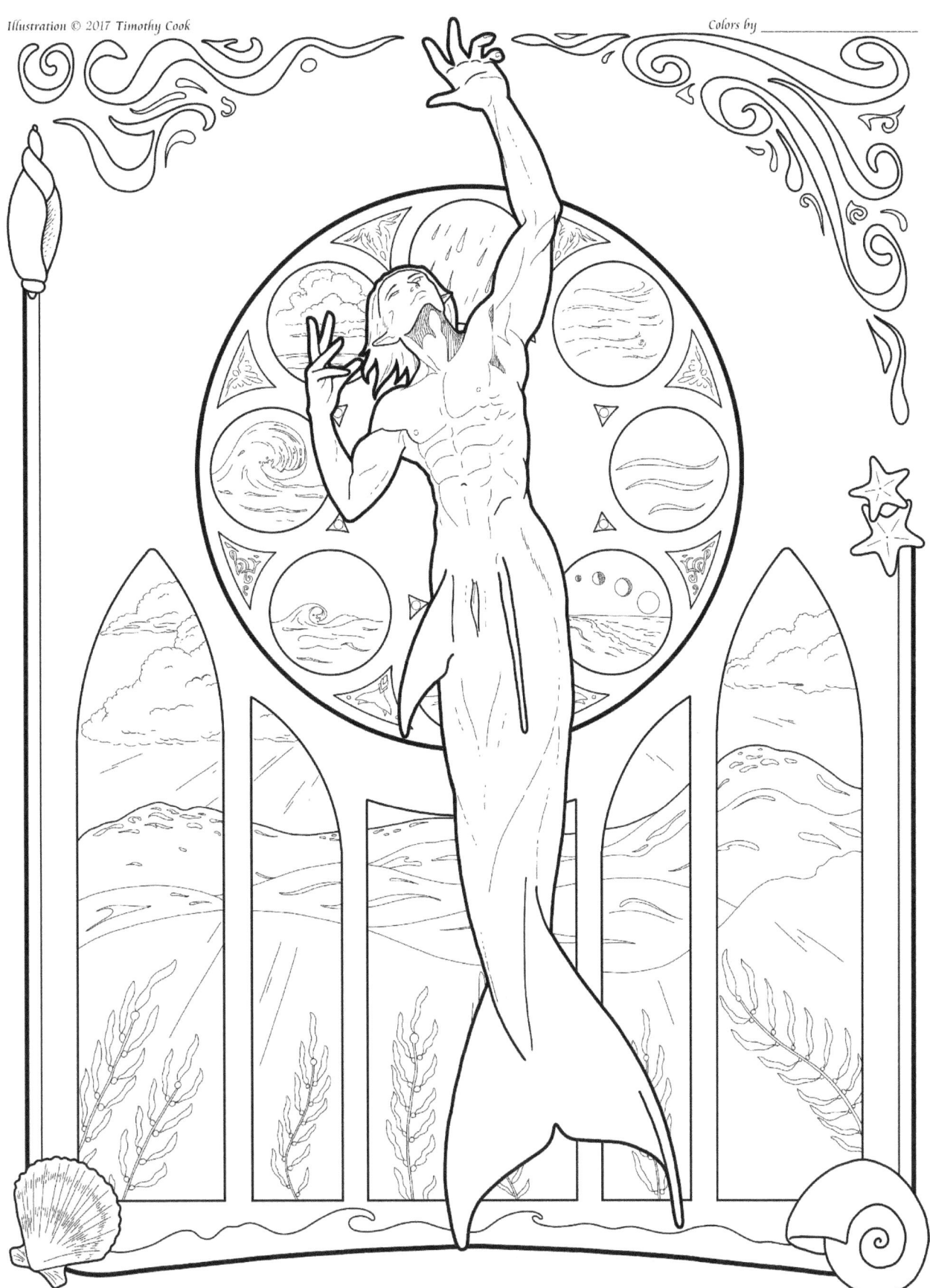

Part II

Colors by _____

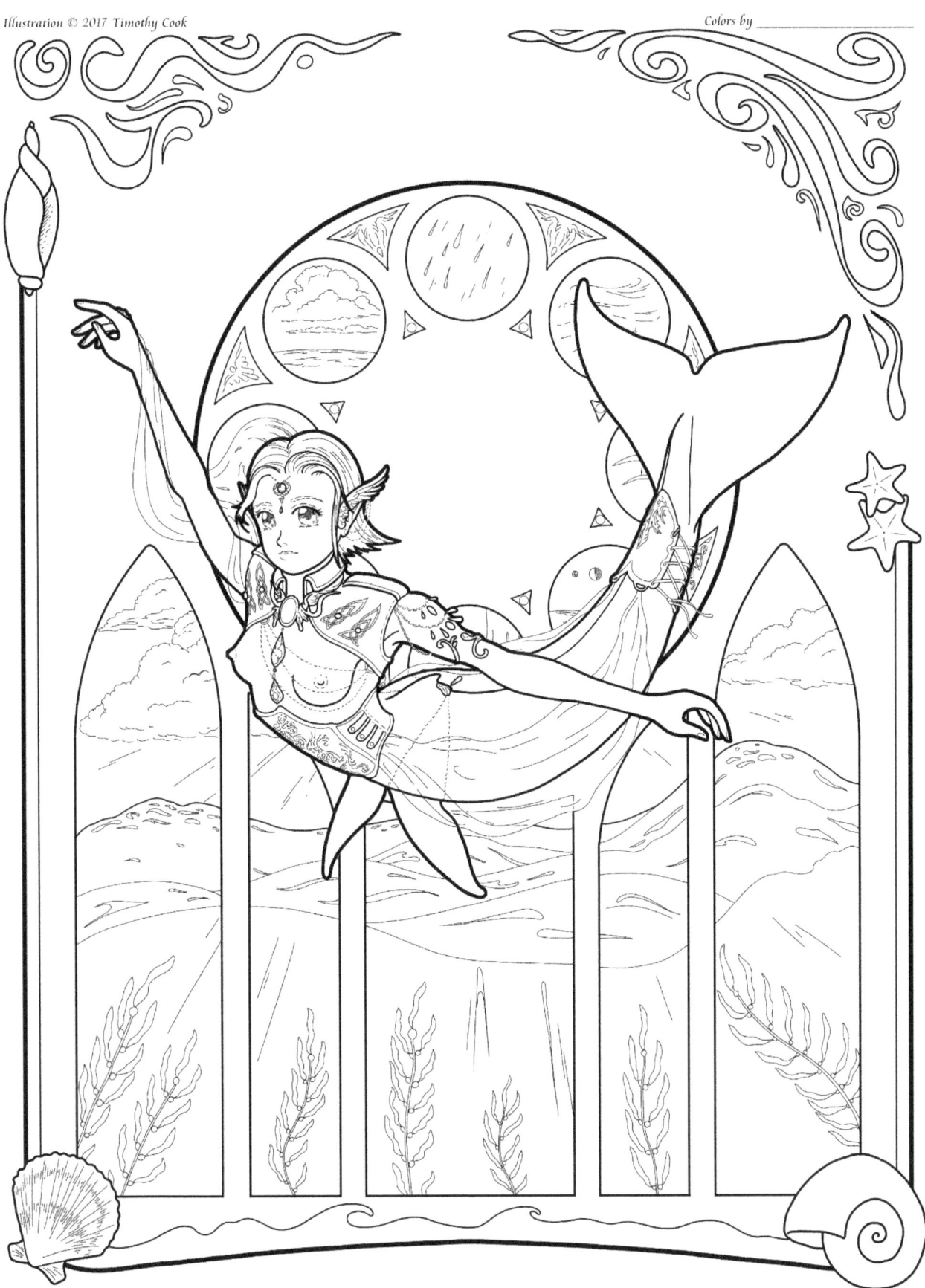

Colors by _____

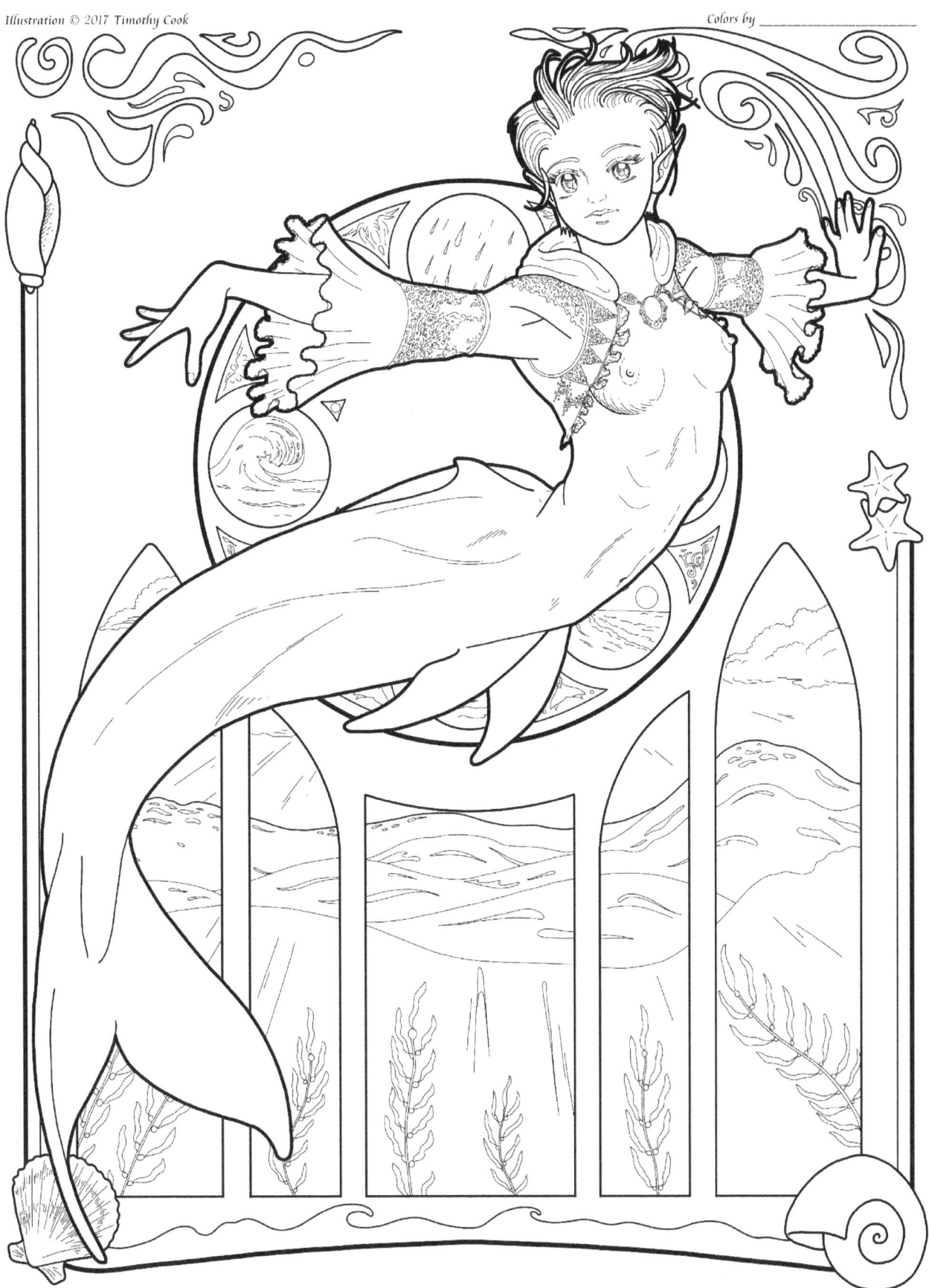

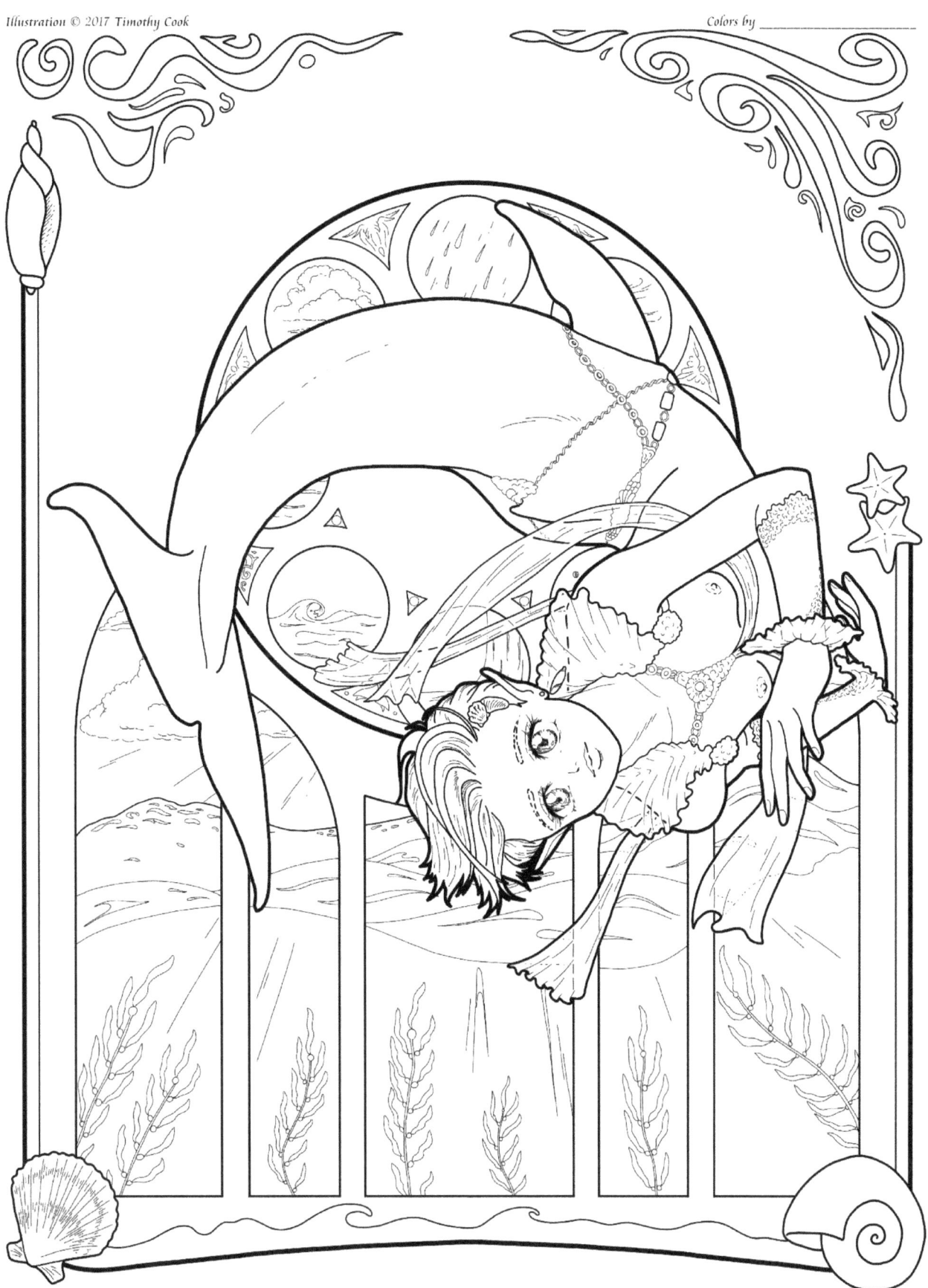

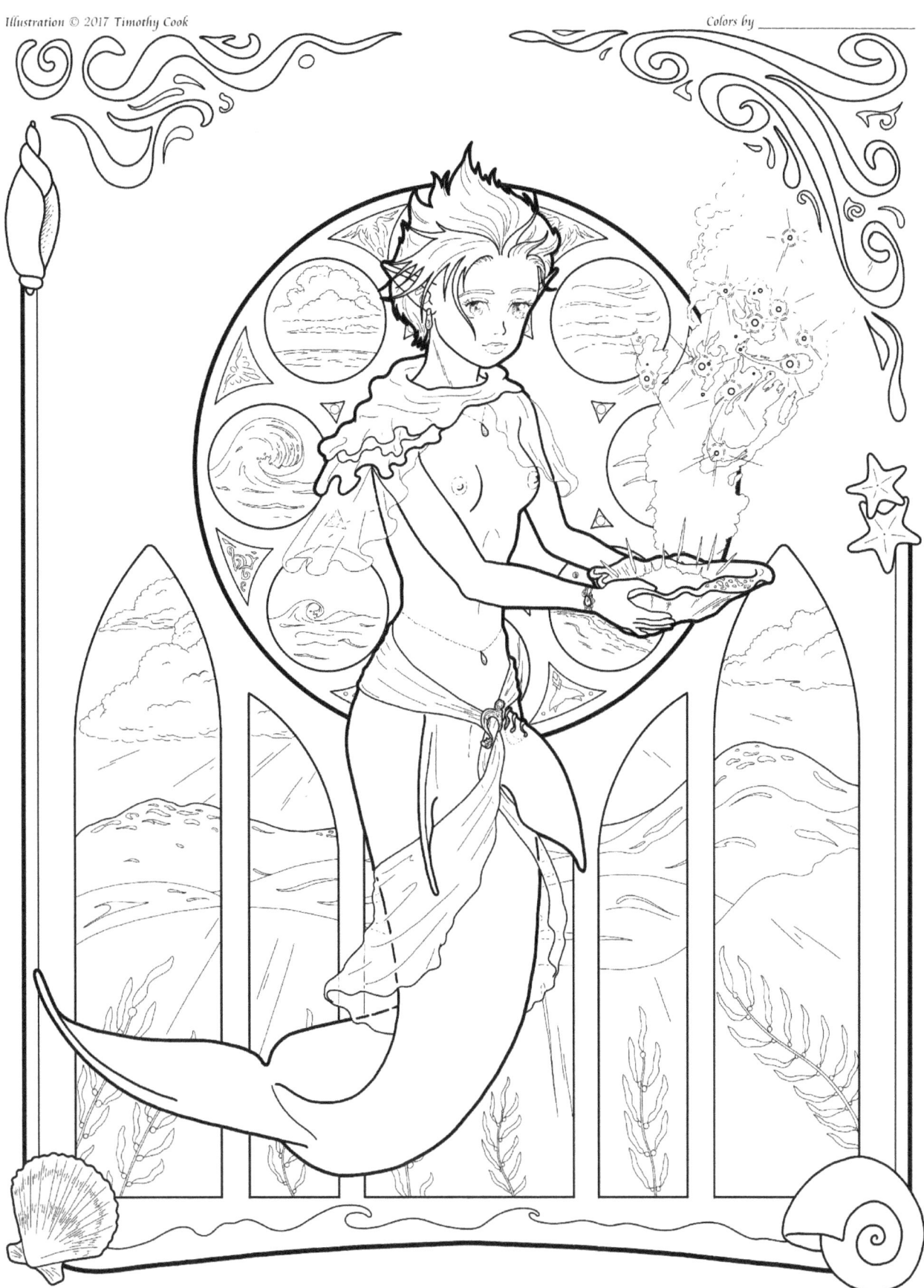

Colors by _____

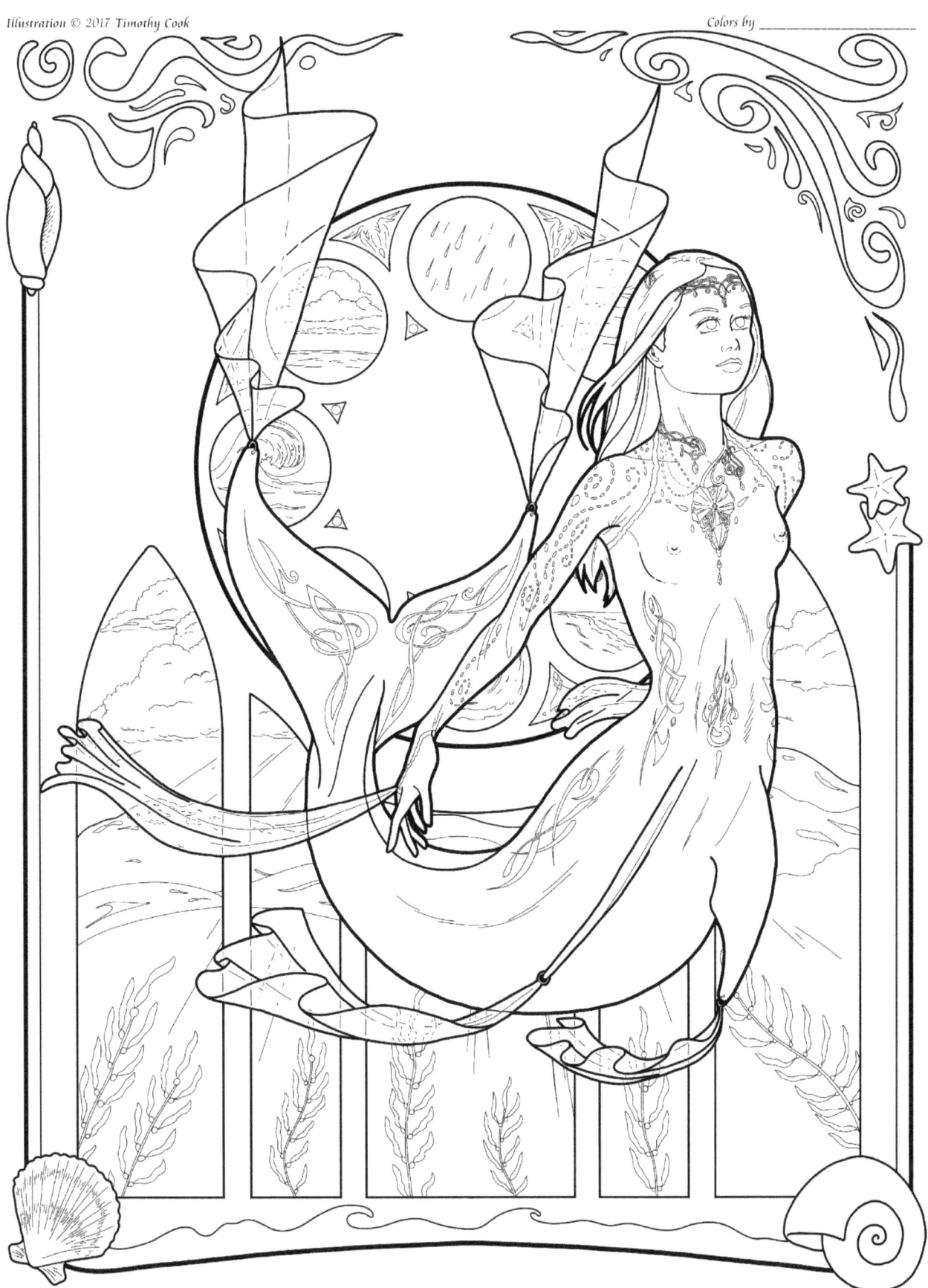

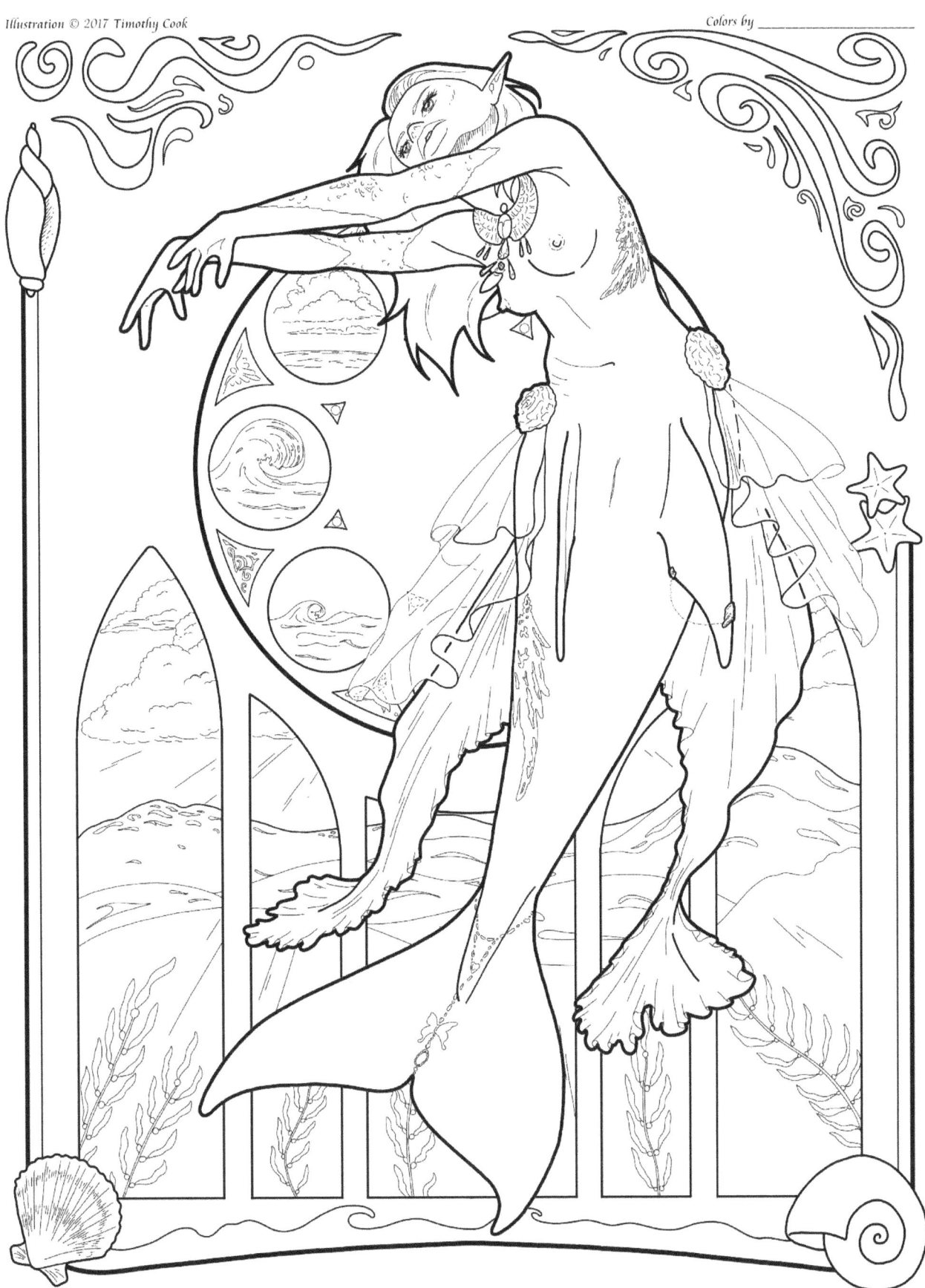

Colors by _____

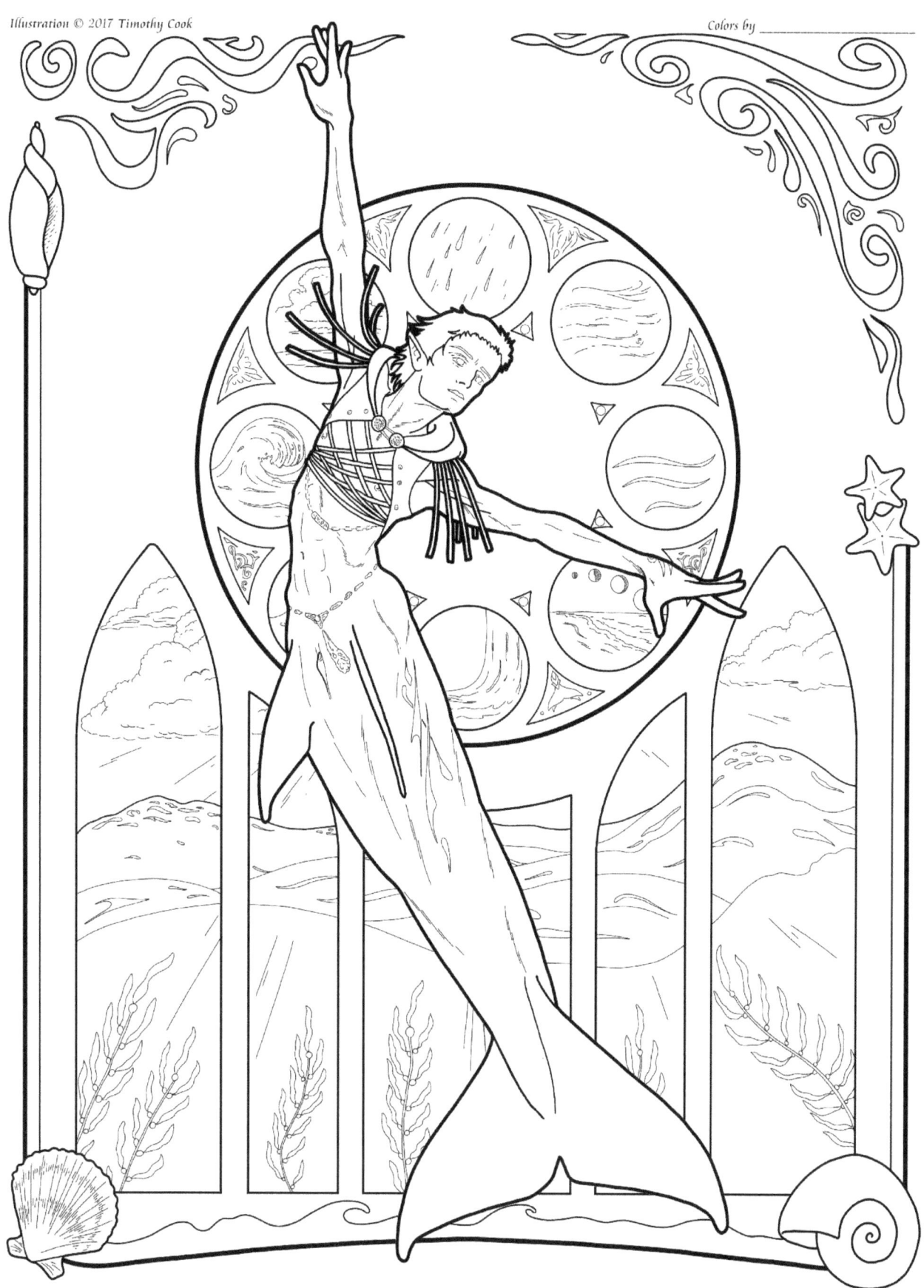

Colors by _____

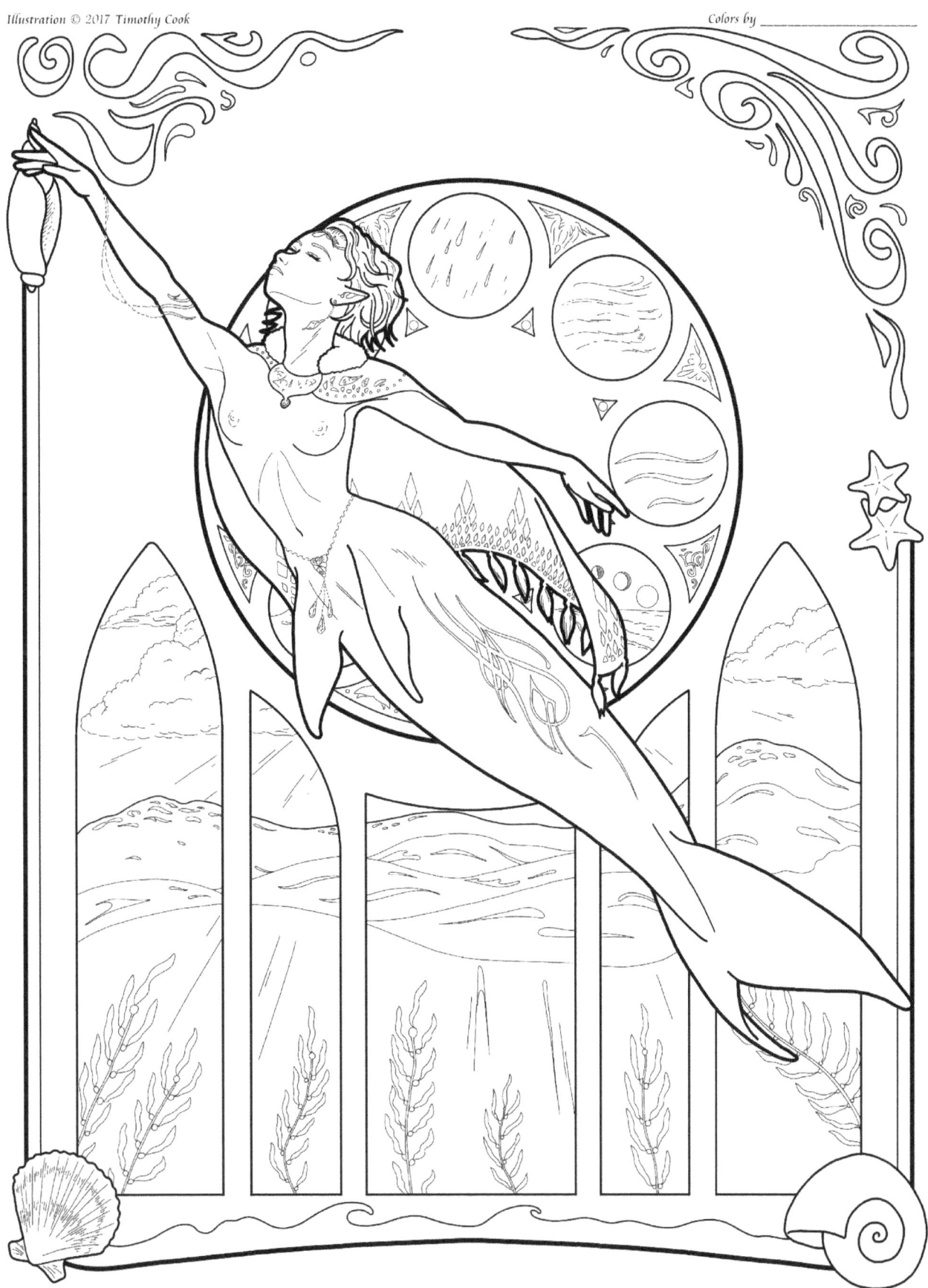

Colors by _____

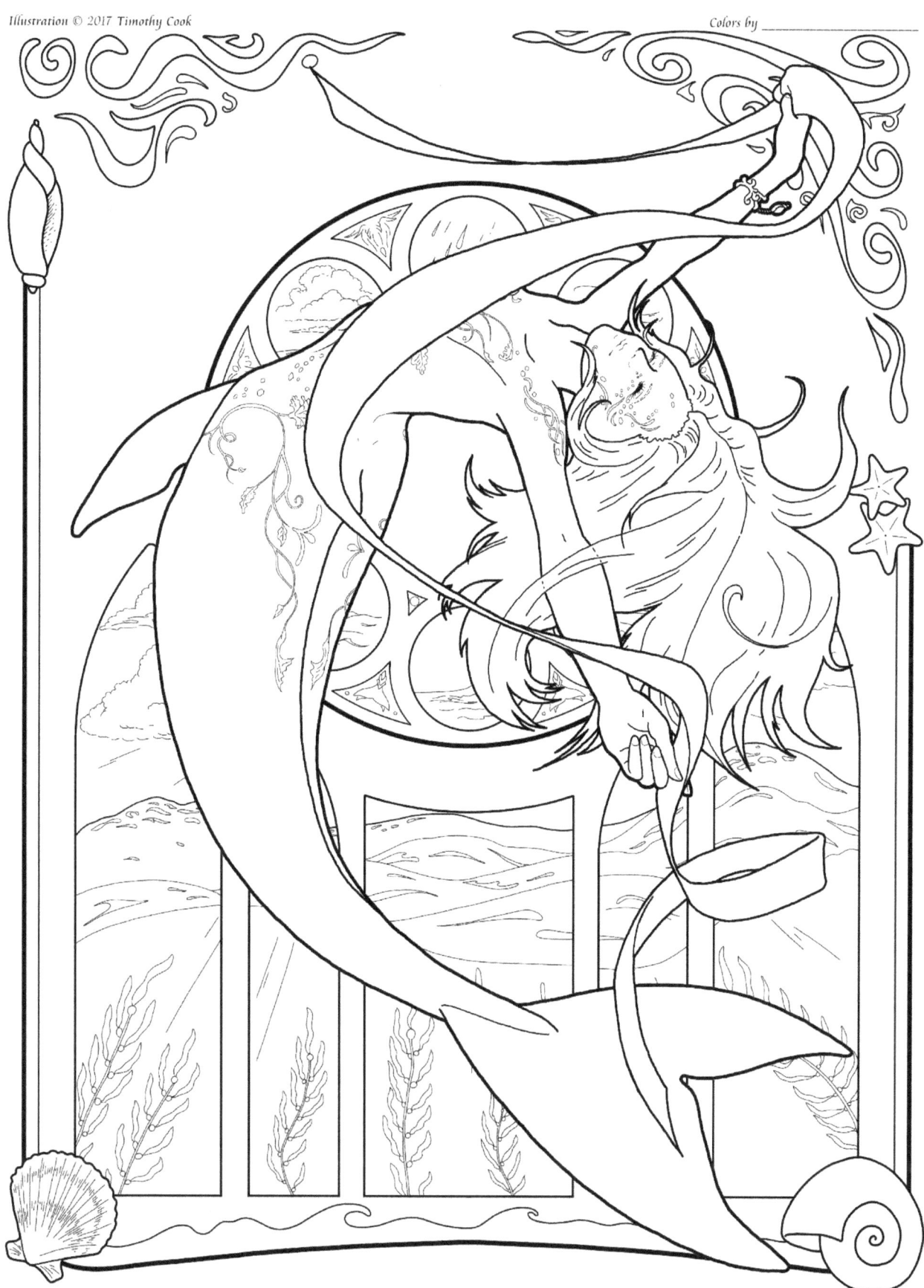

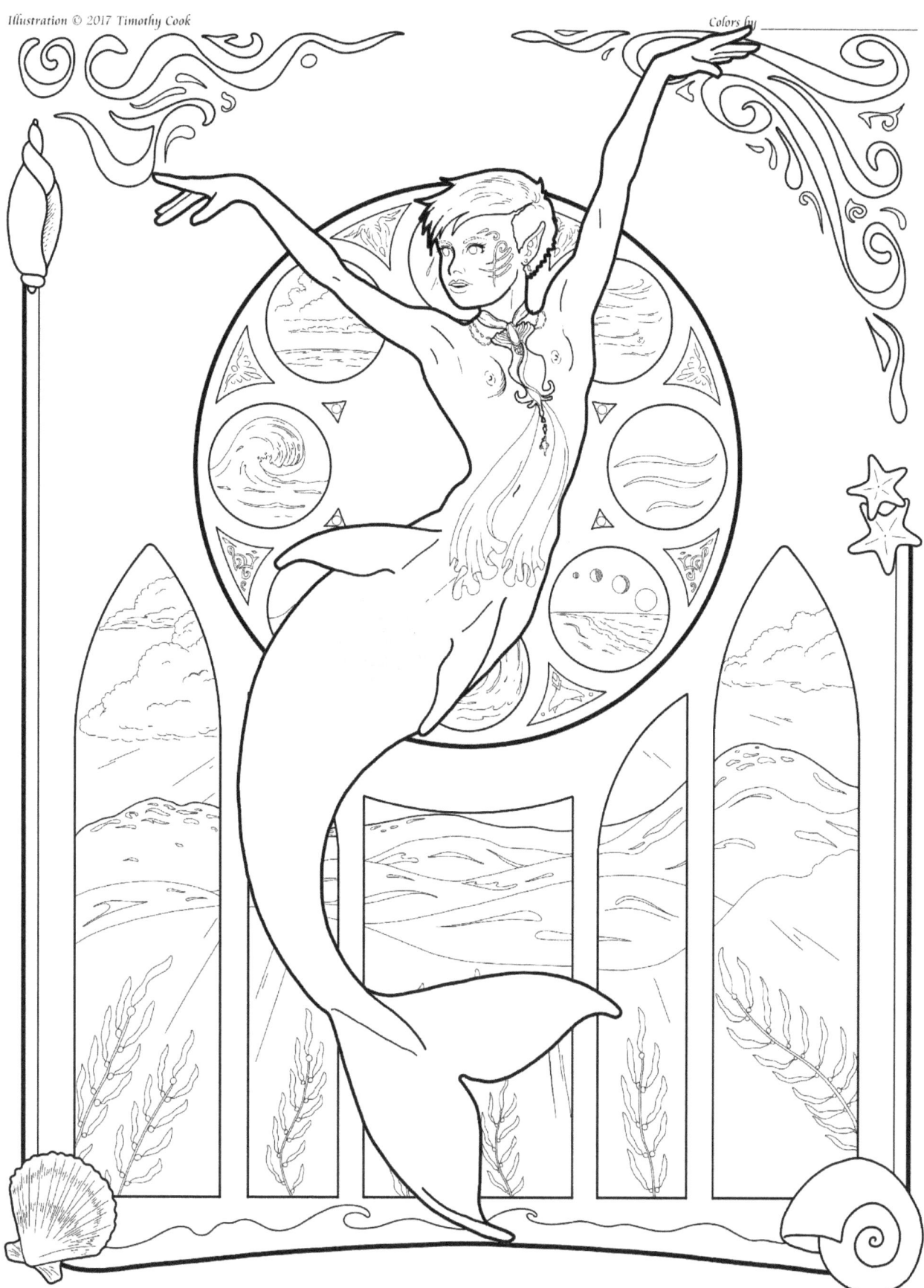

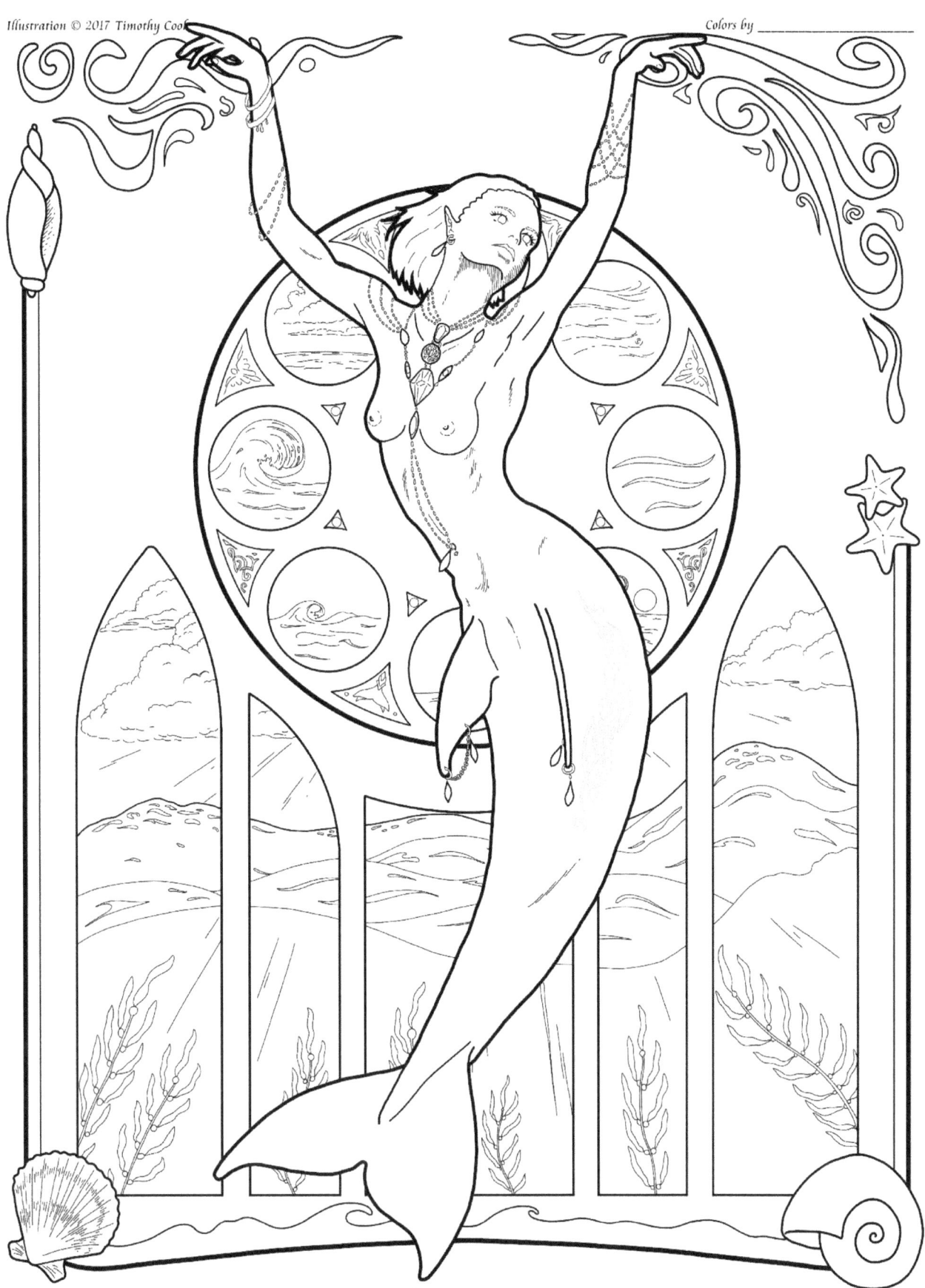

Colors by _____

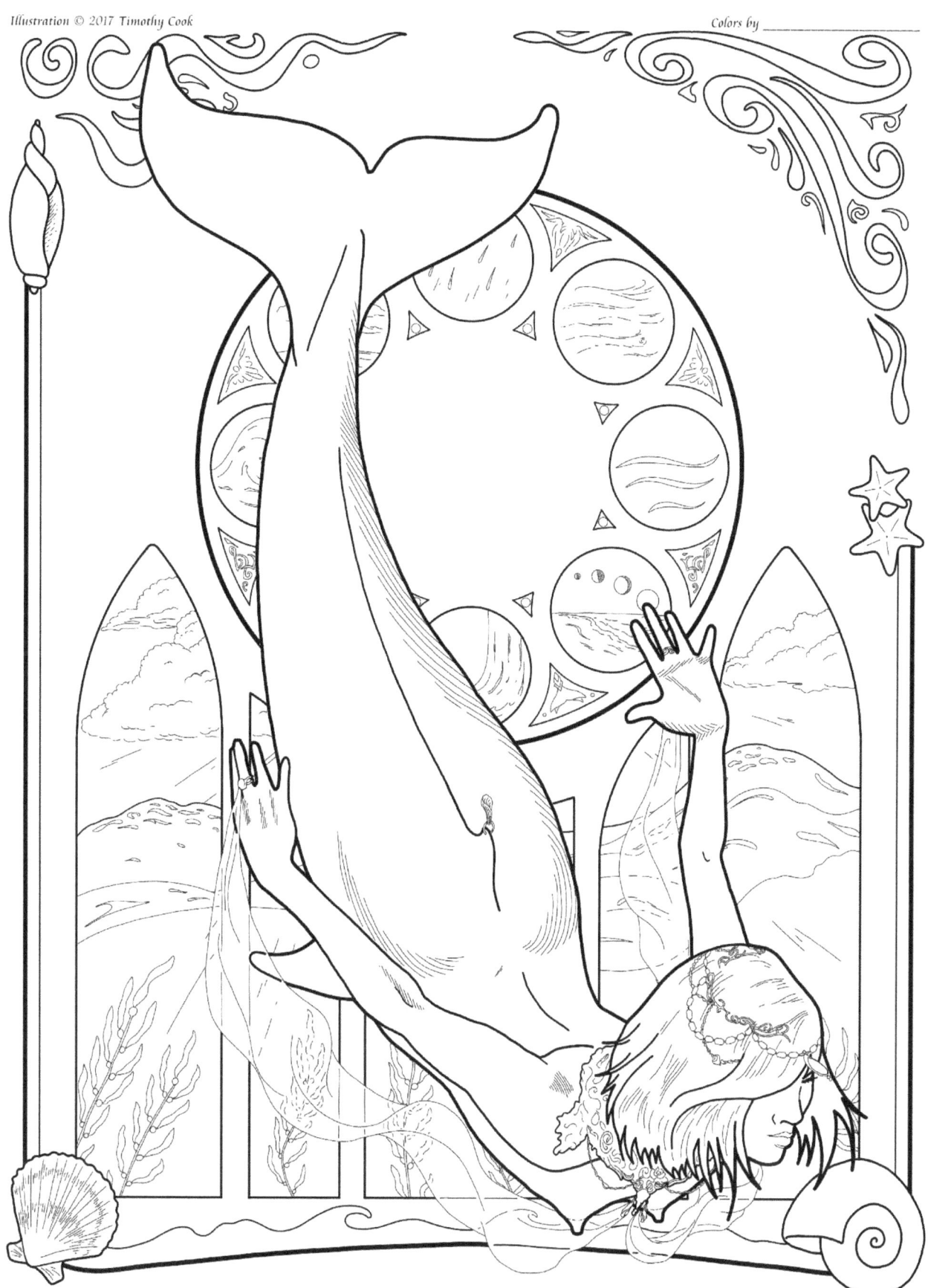

Colors by _____

Part III

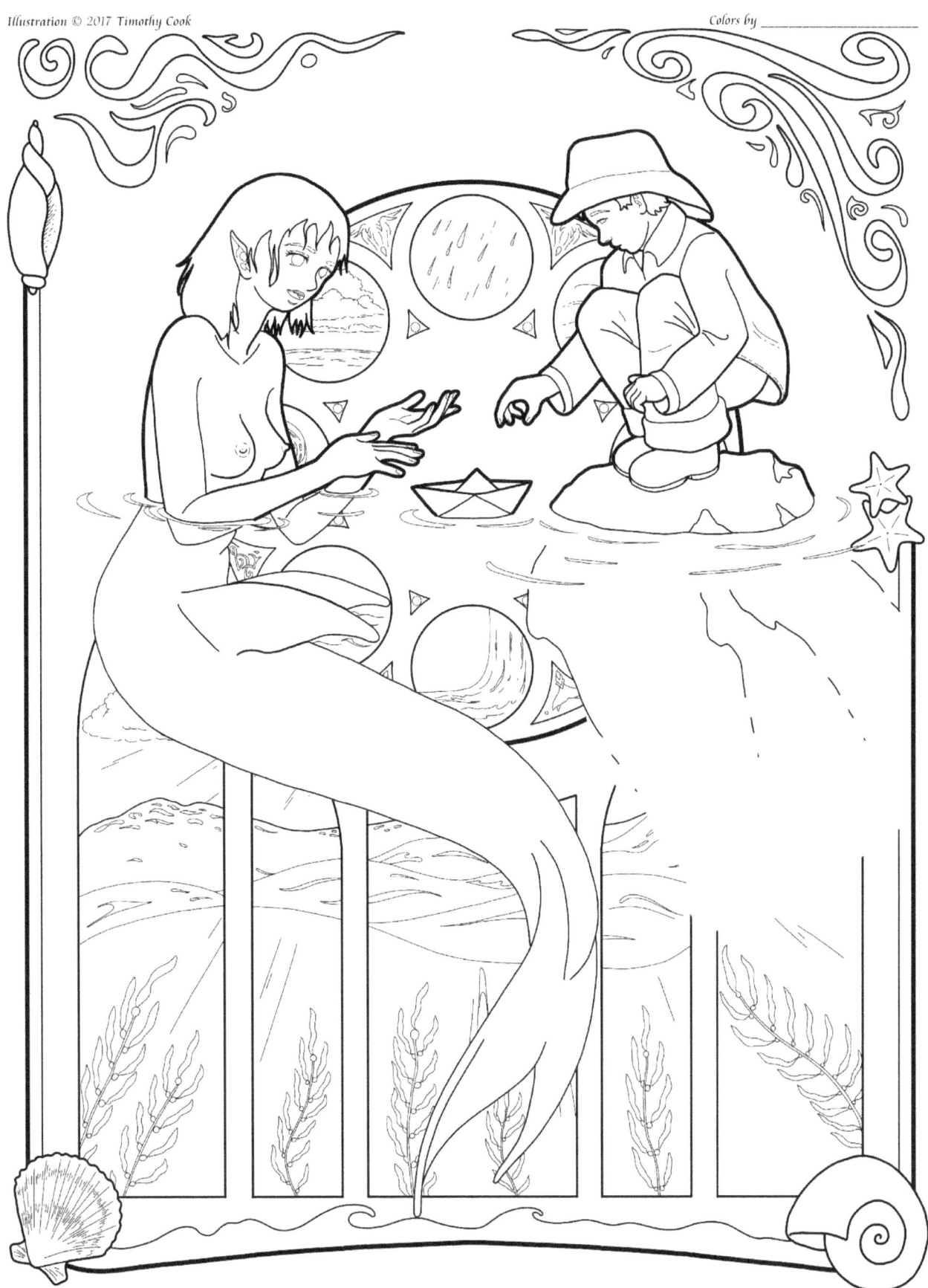

Colors by _____

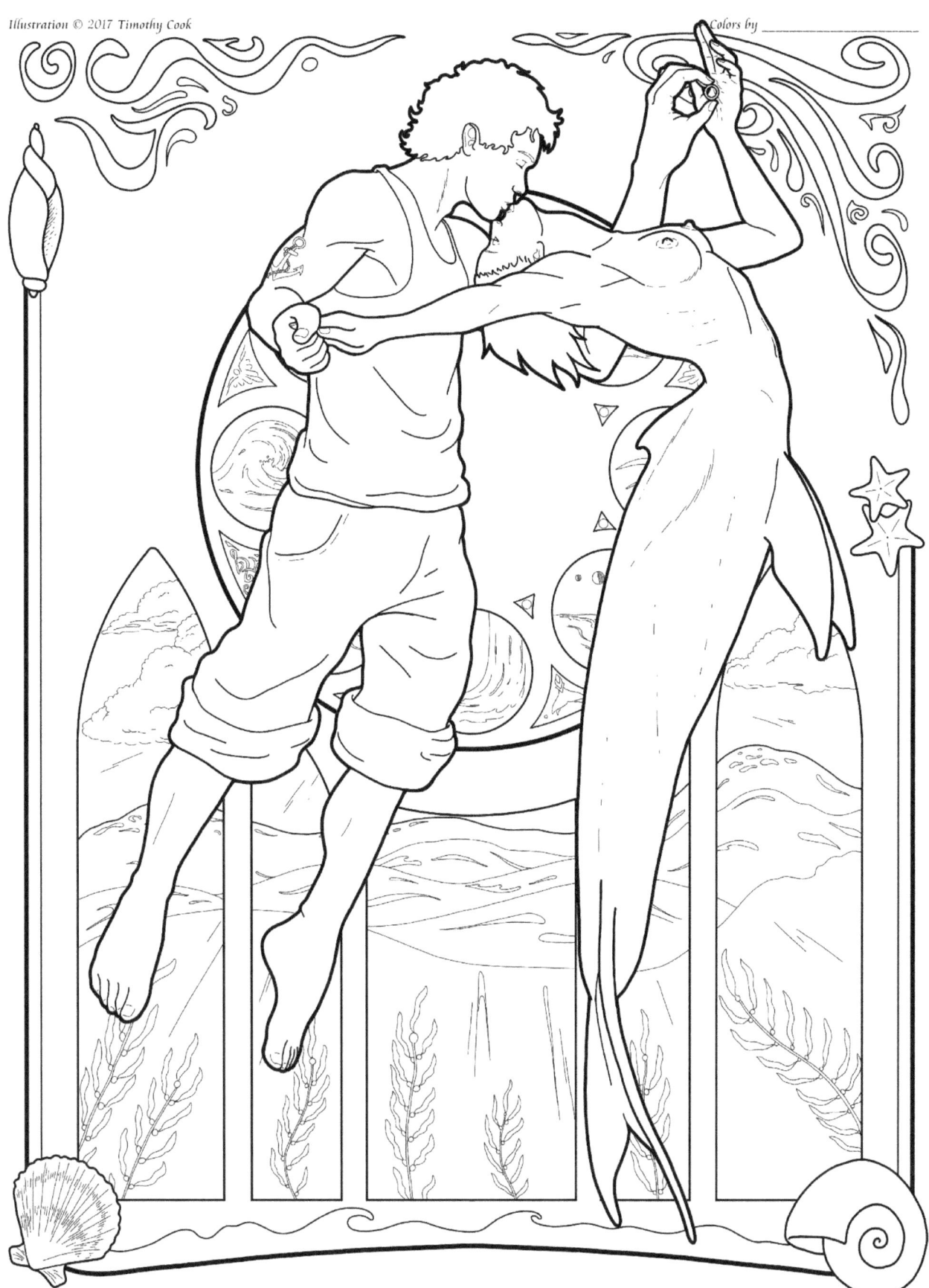

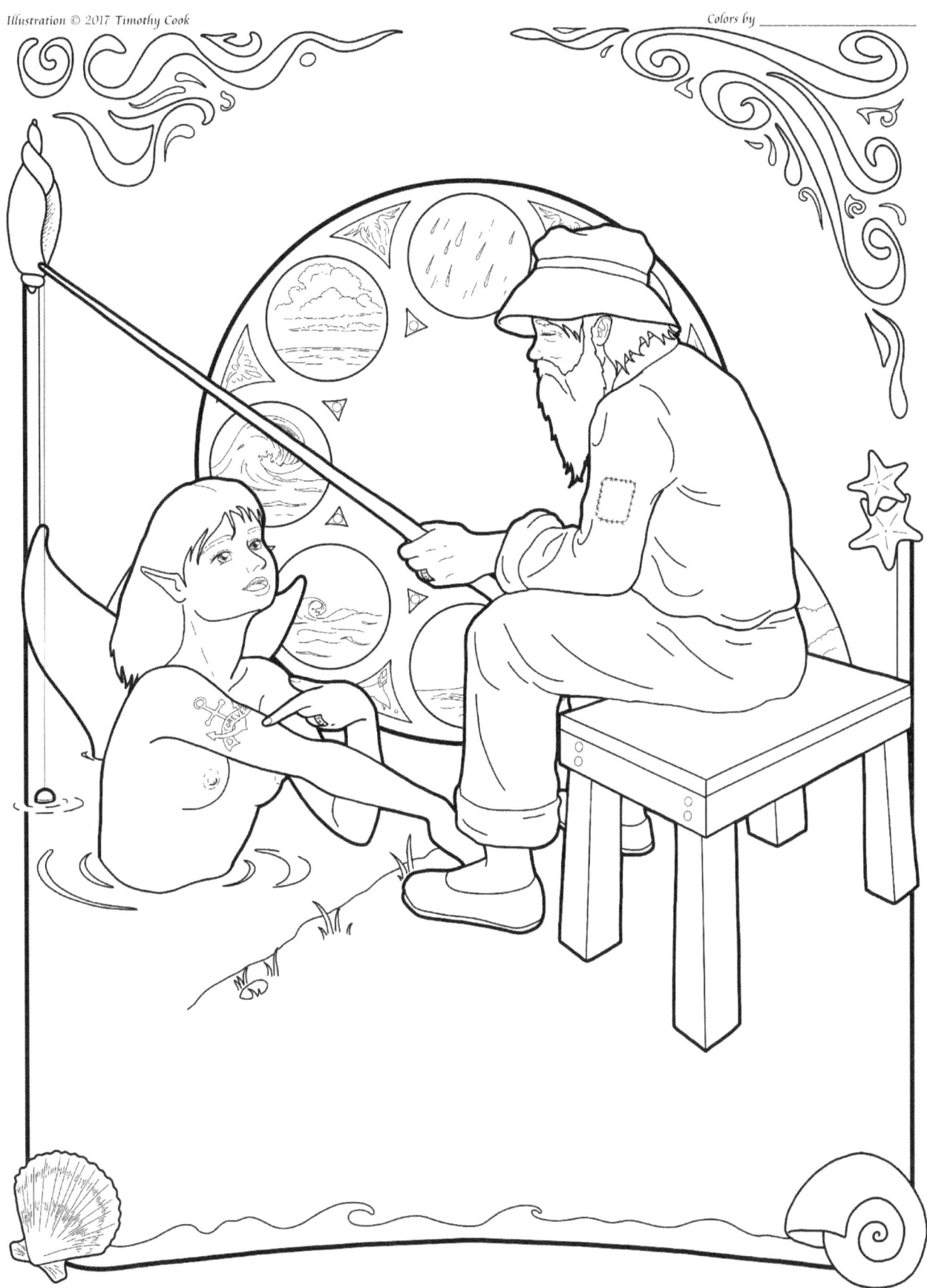

Colors by _____

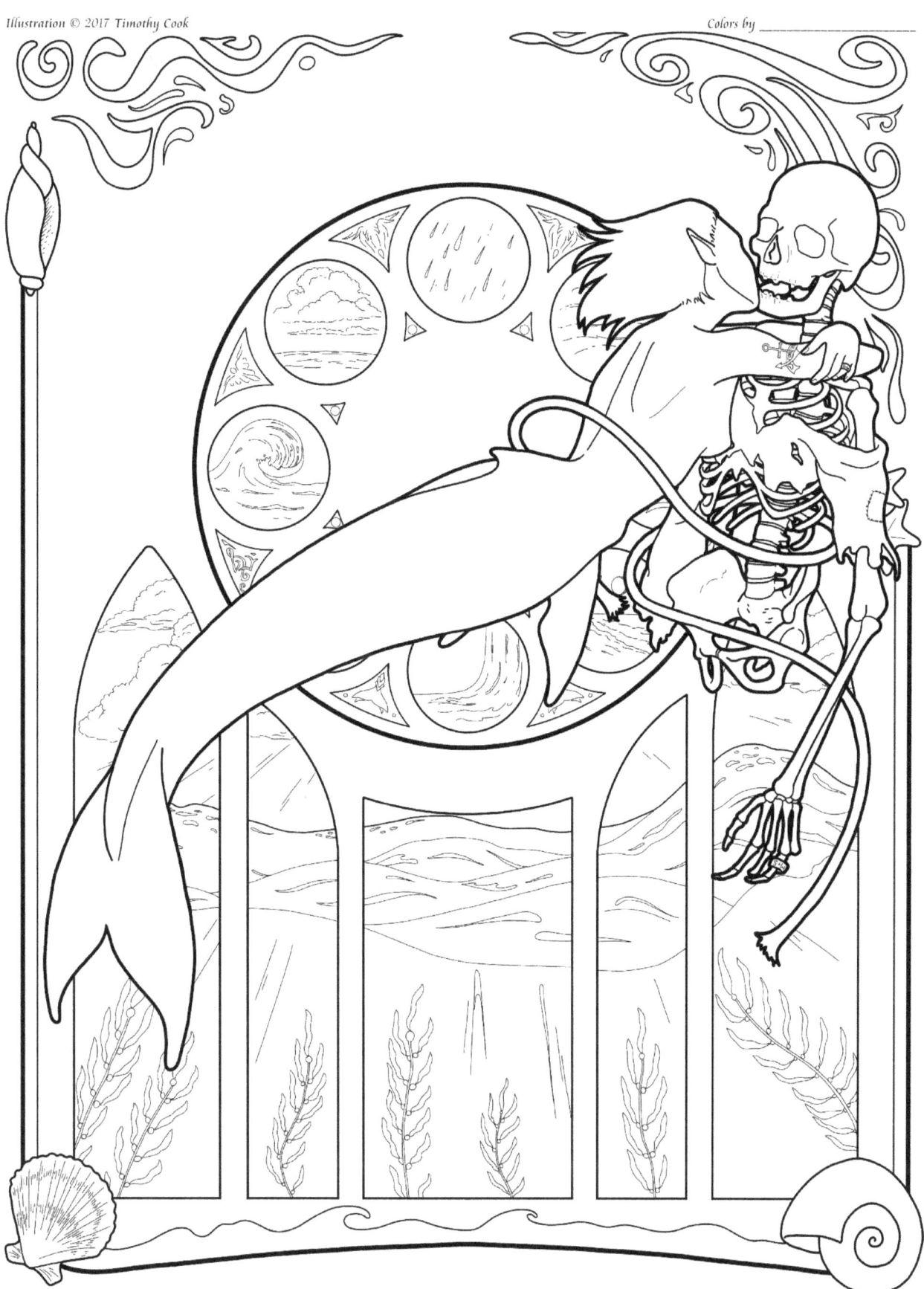

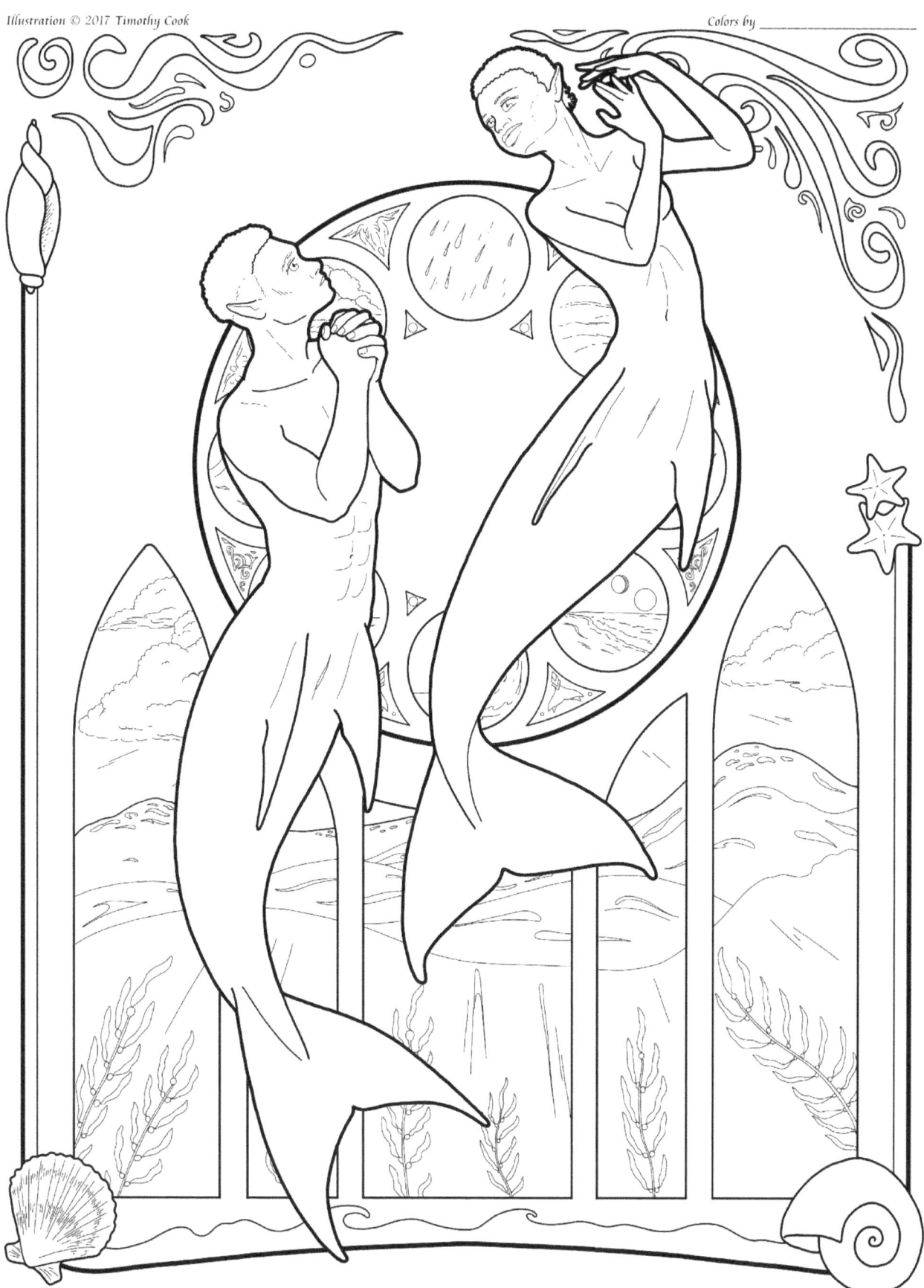

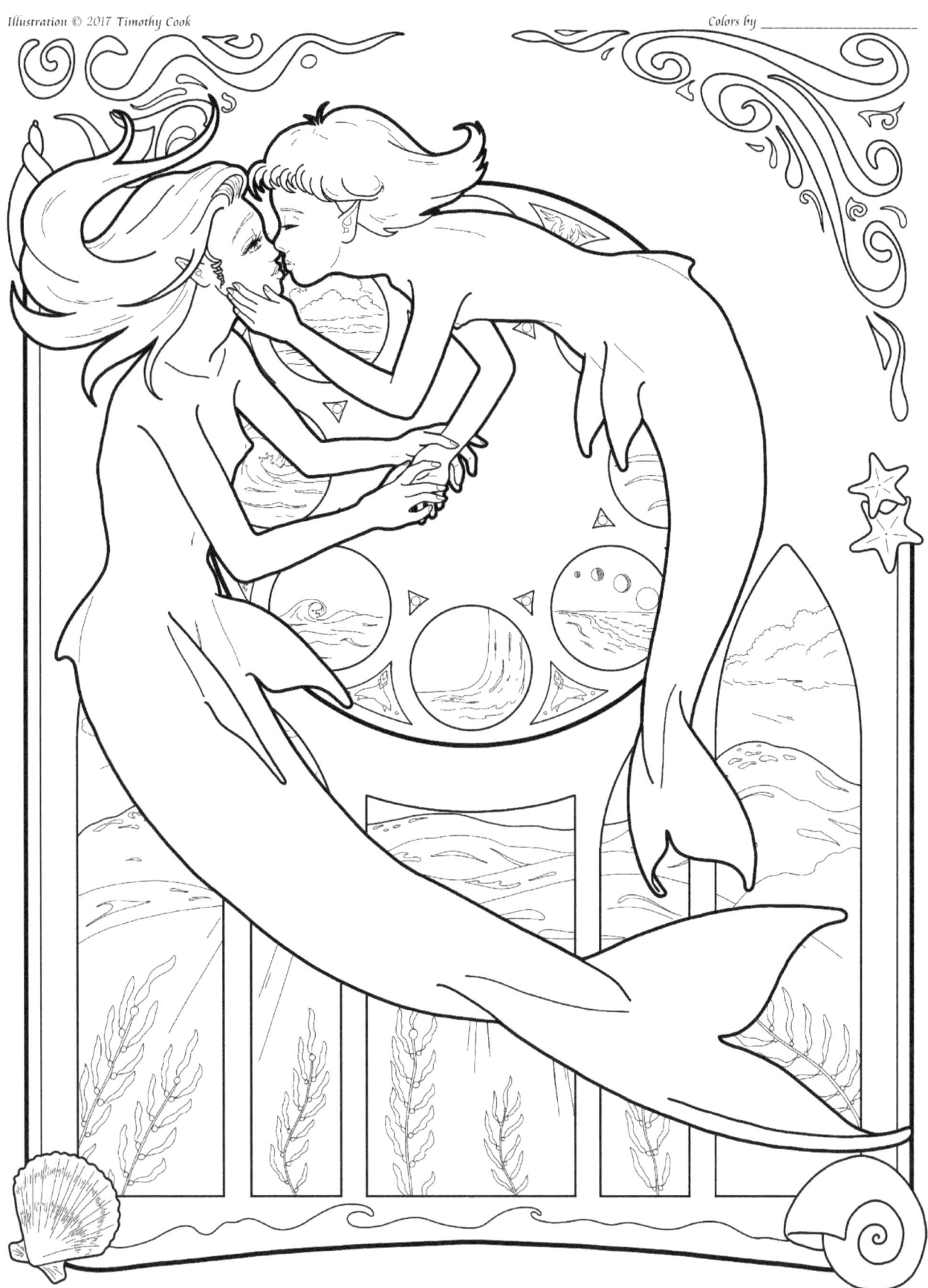

Colors by _____

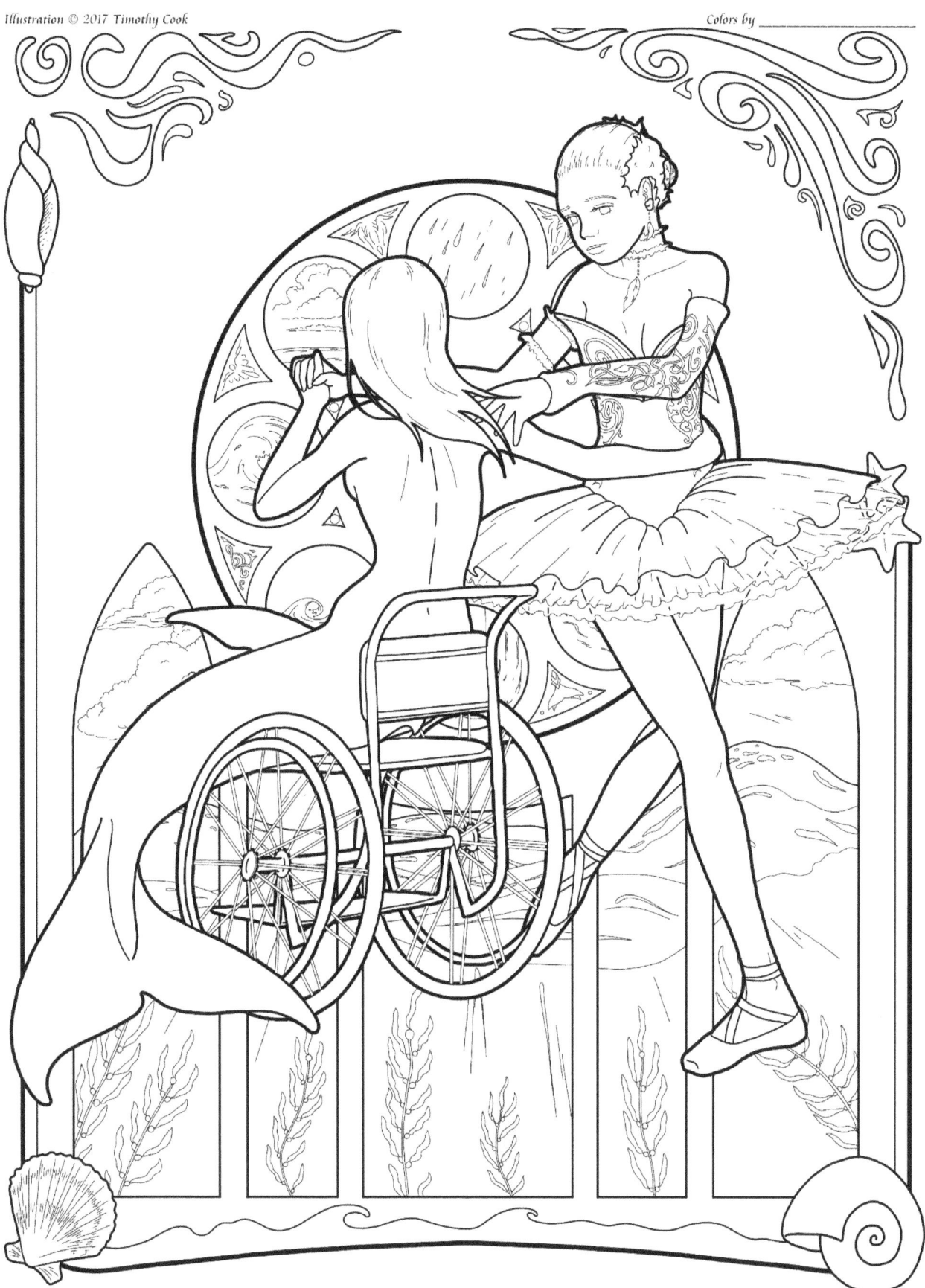

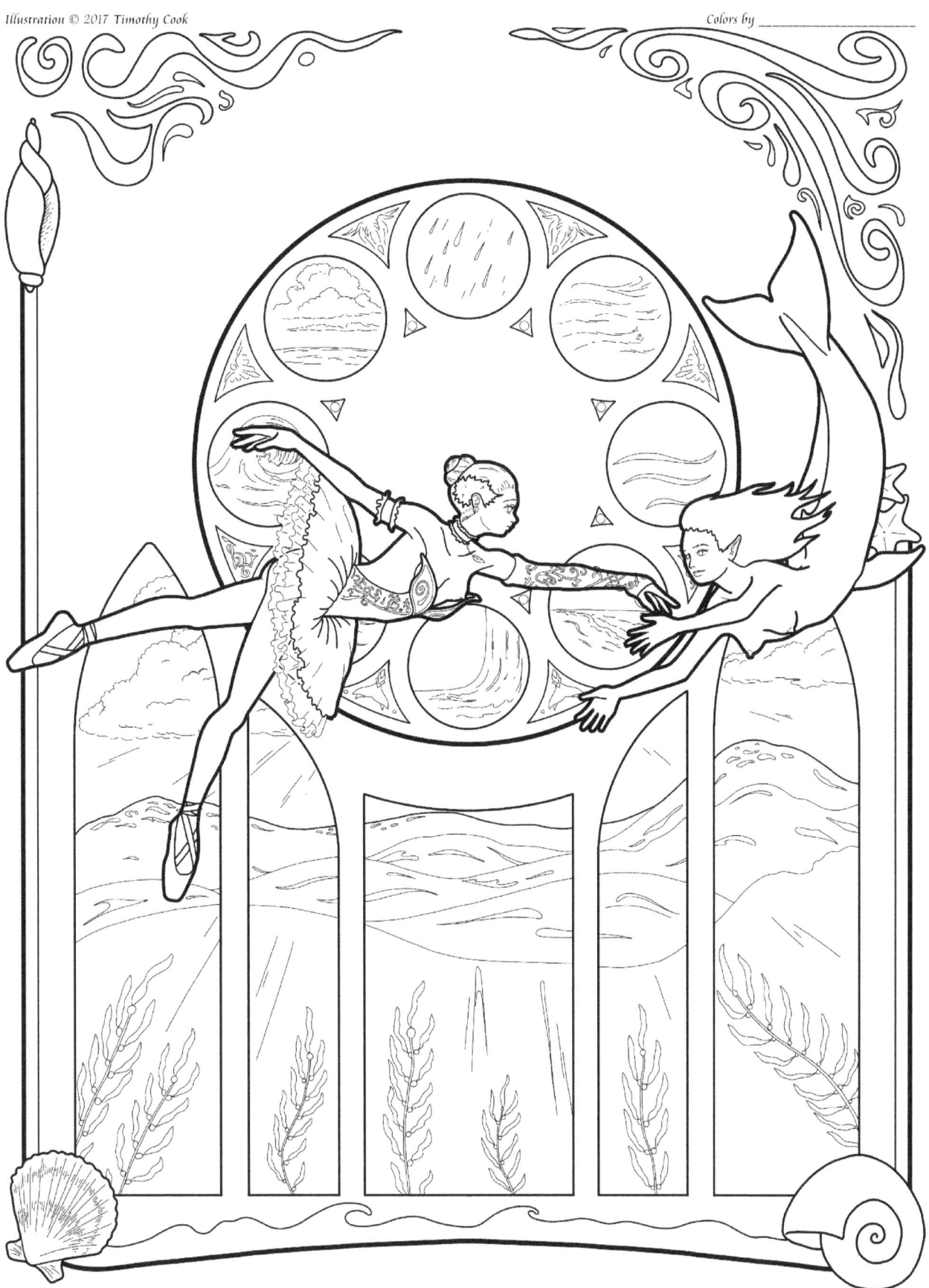

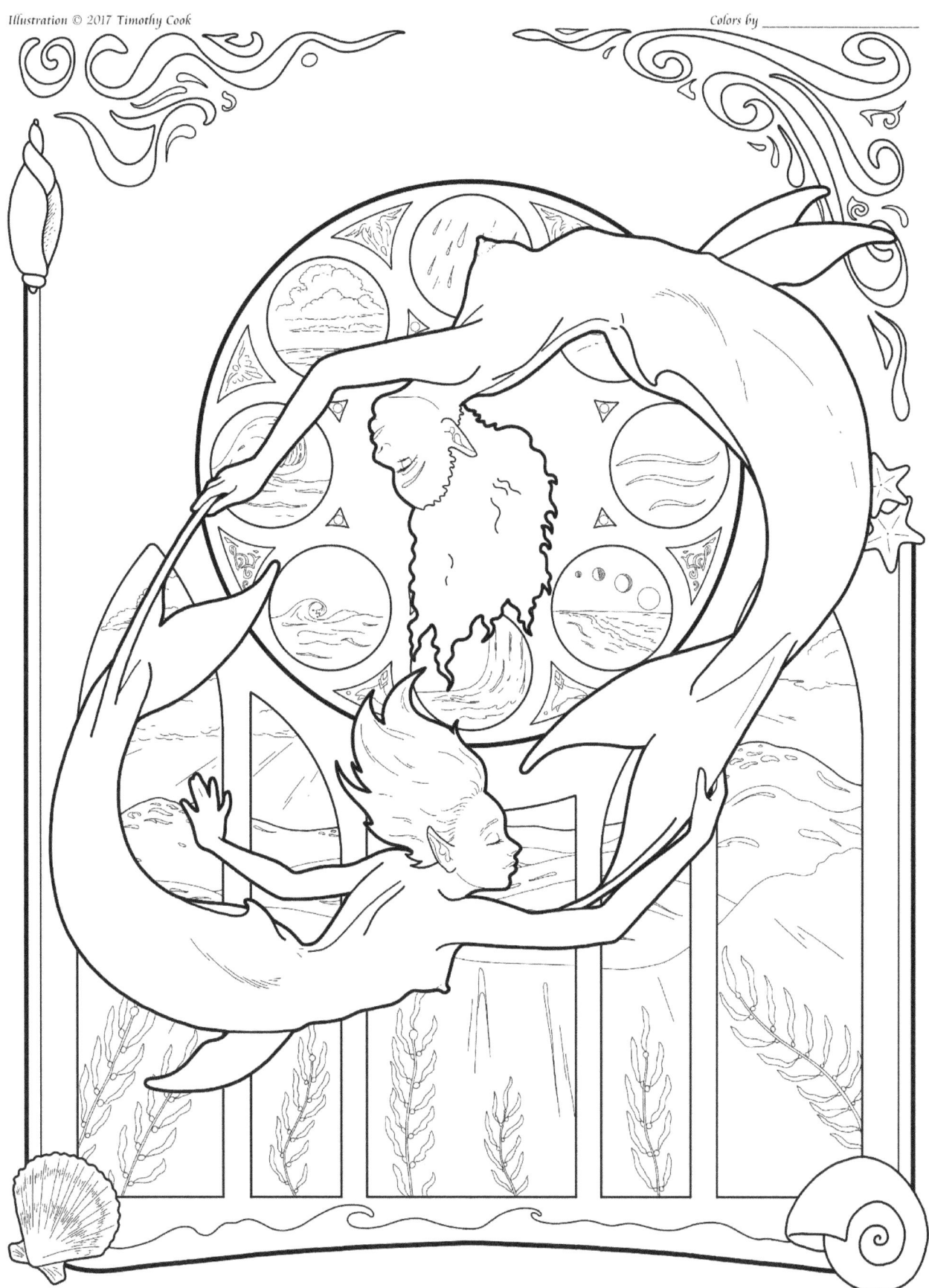

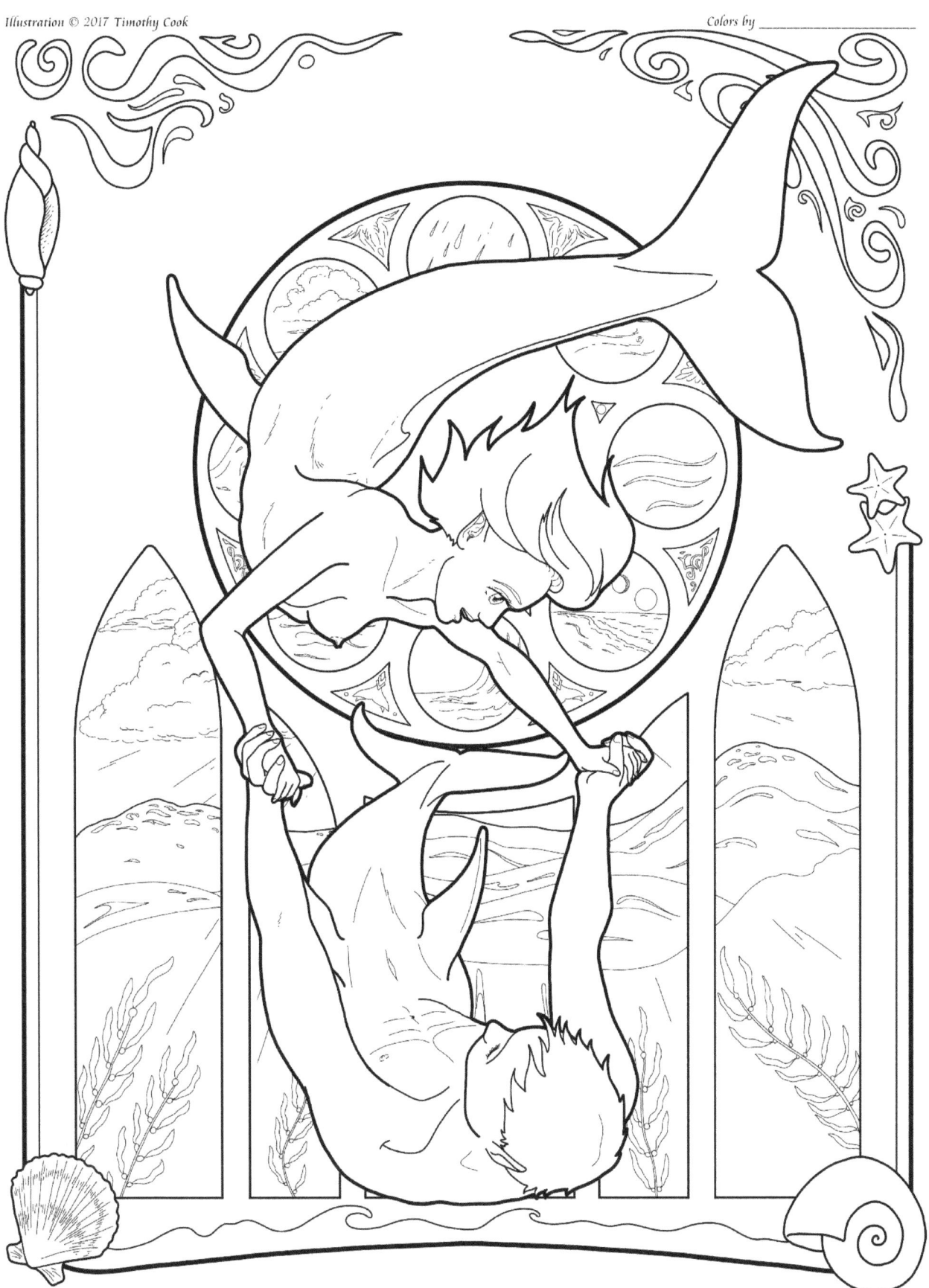

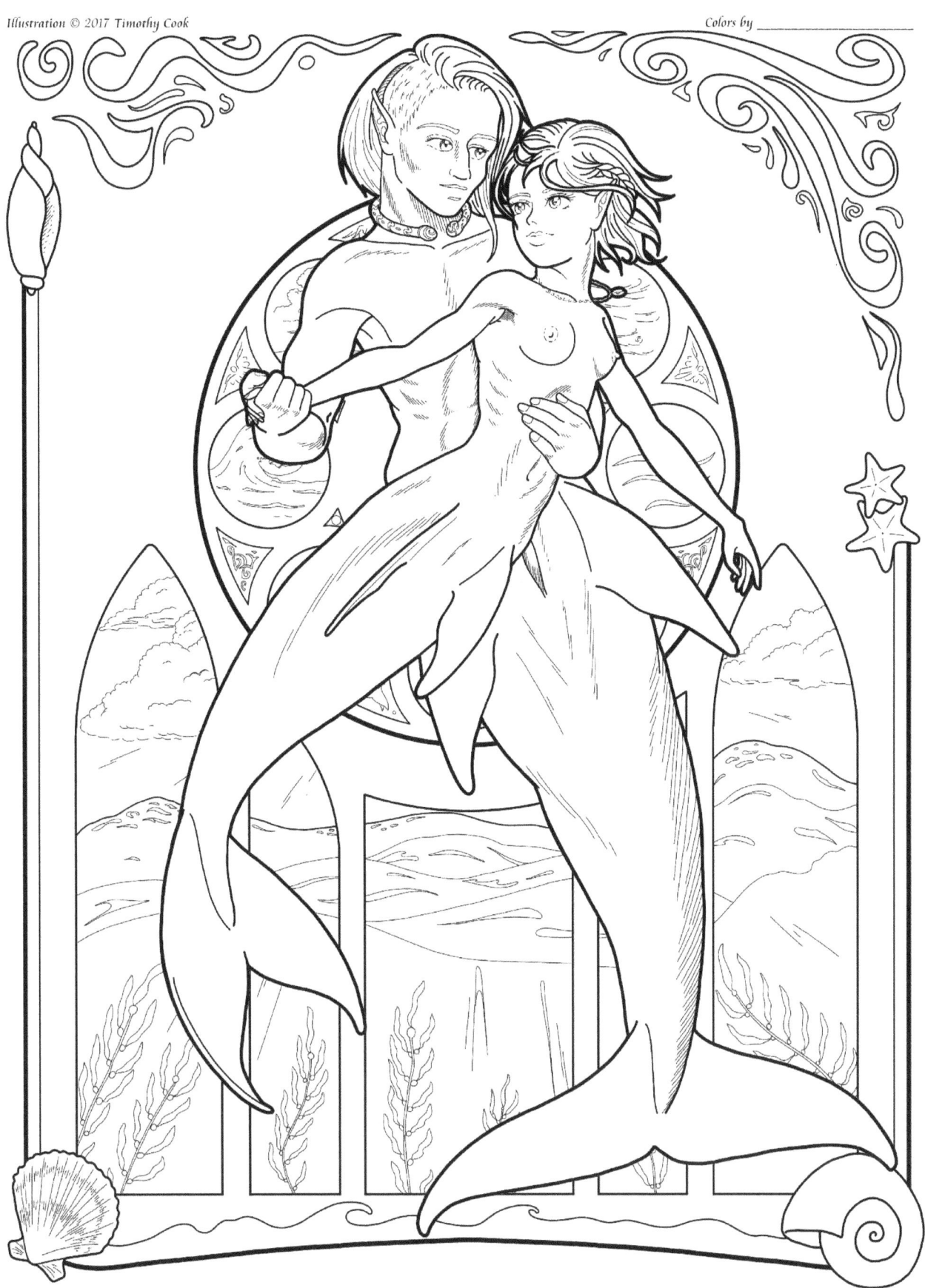

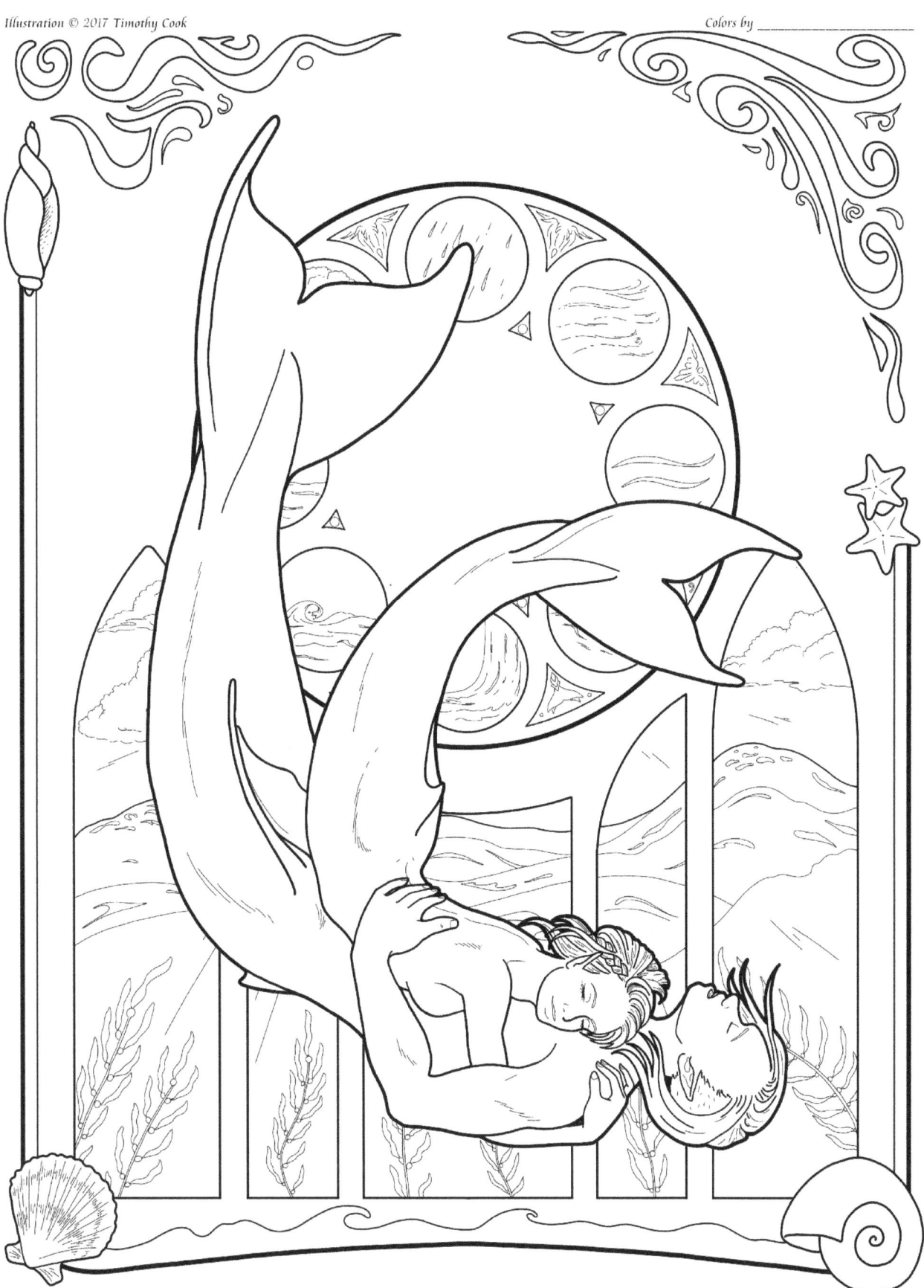

Part IV

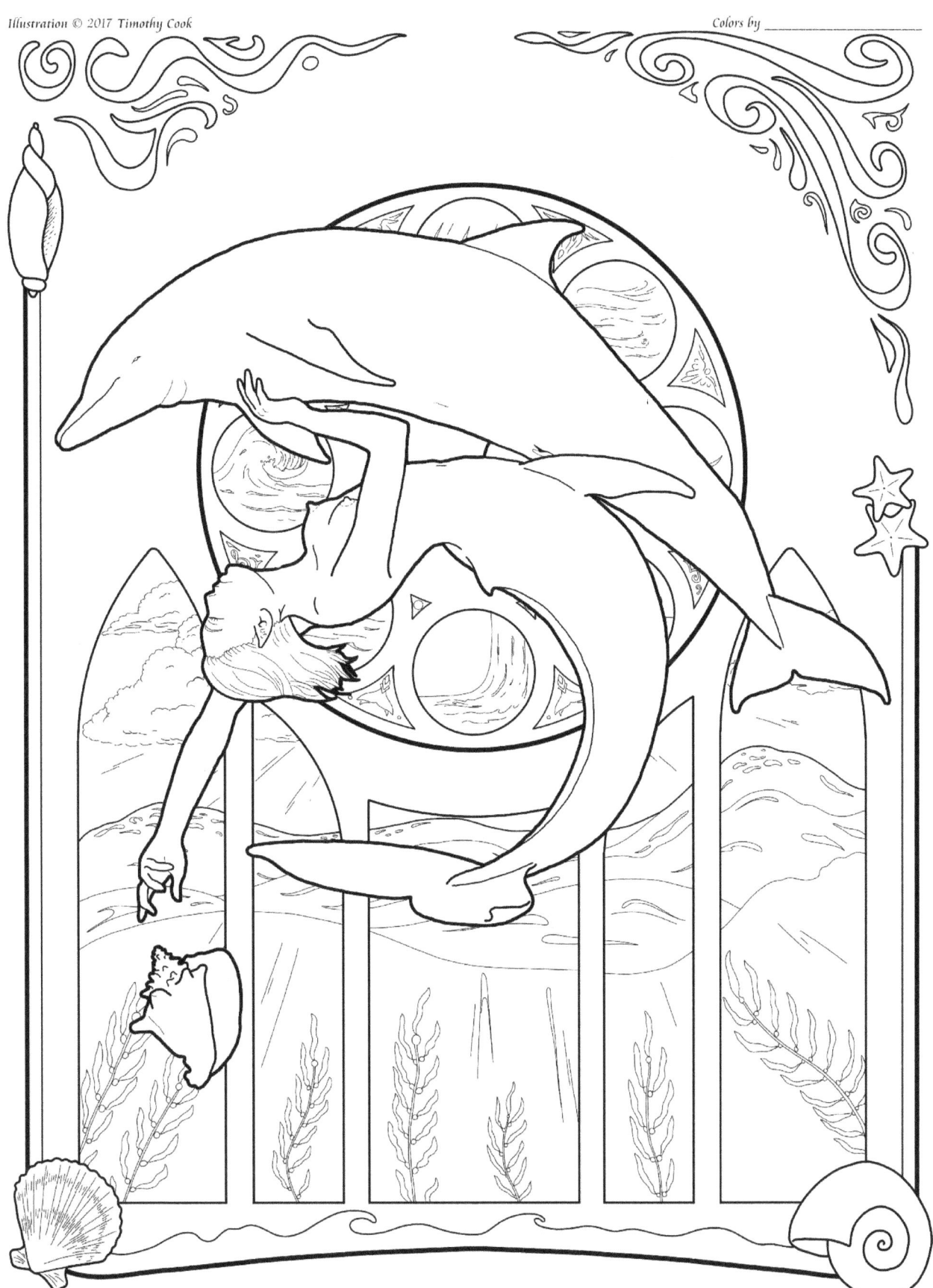

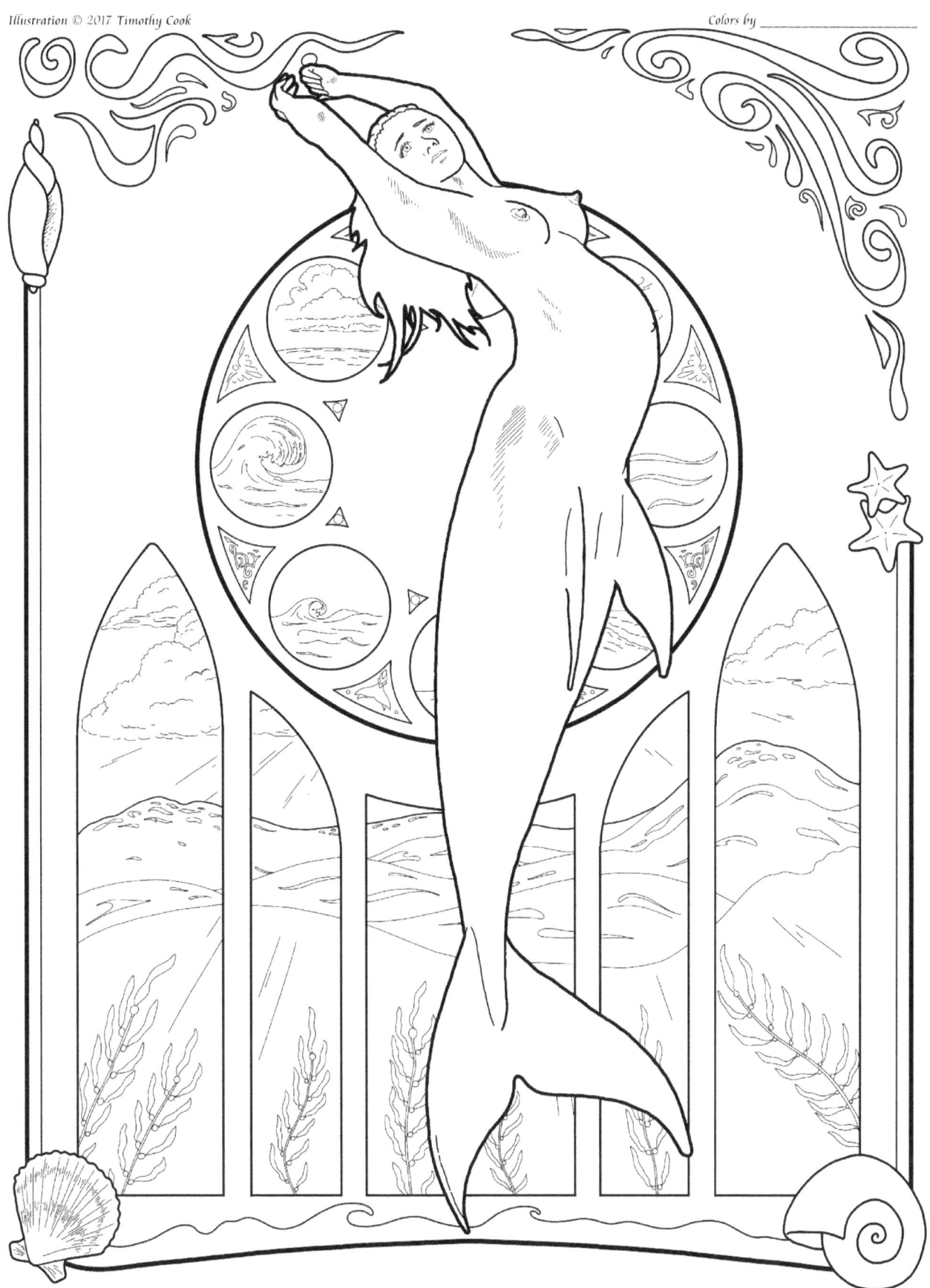

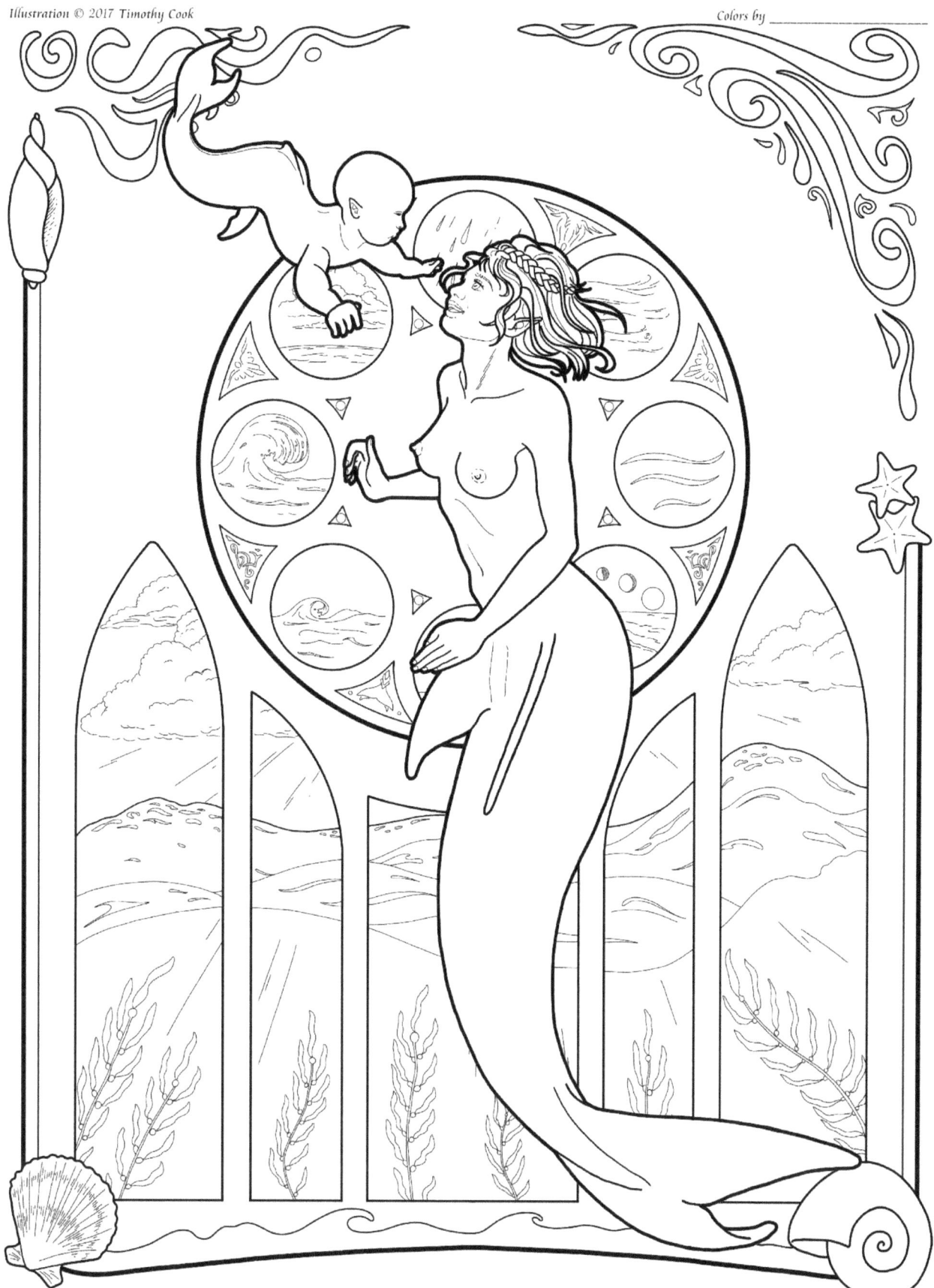

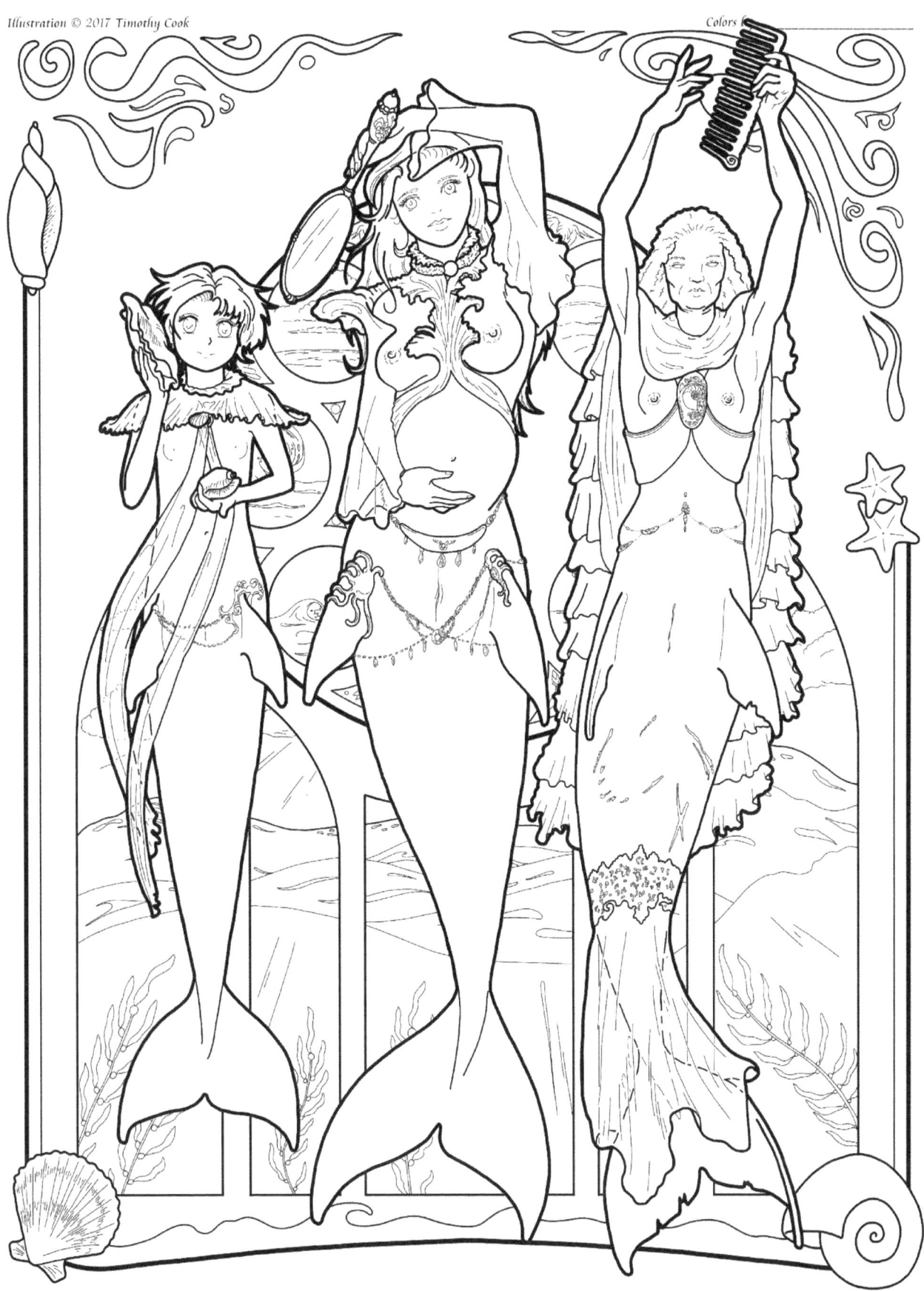

Colors by _____

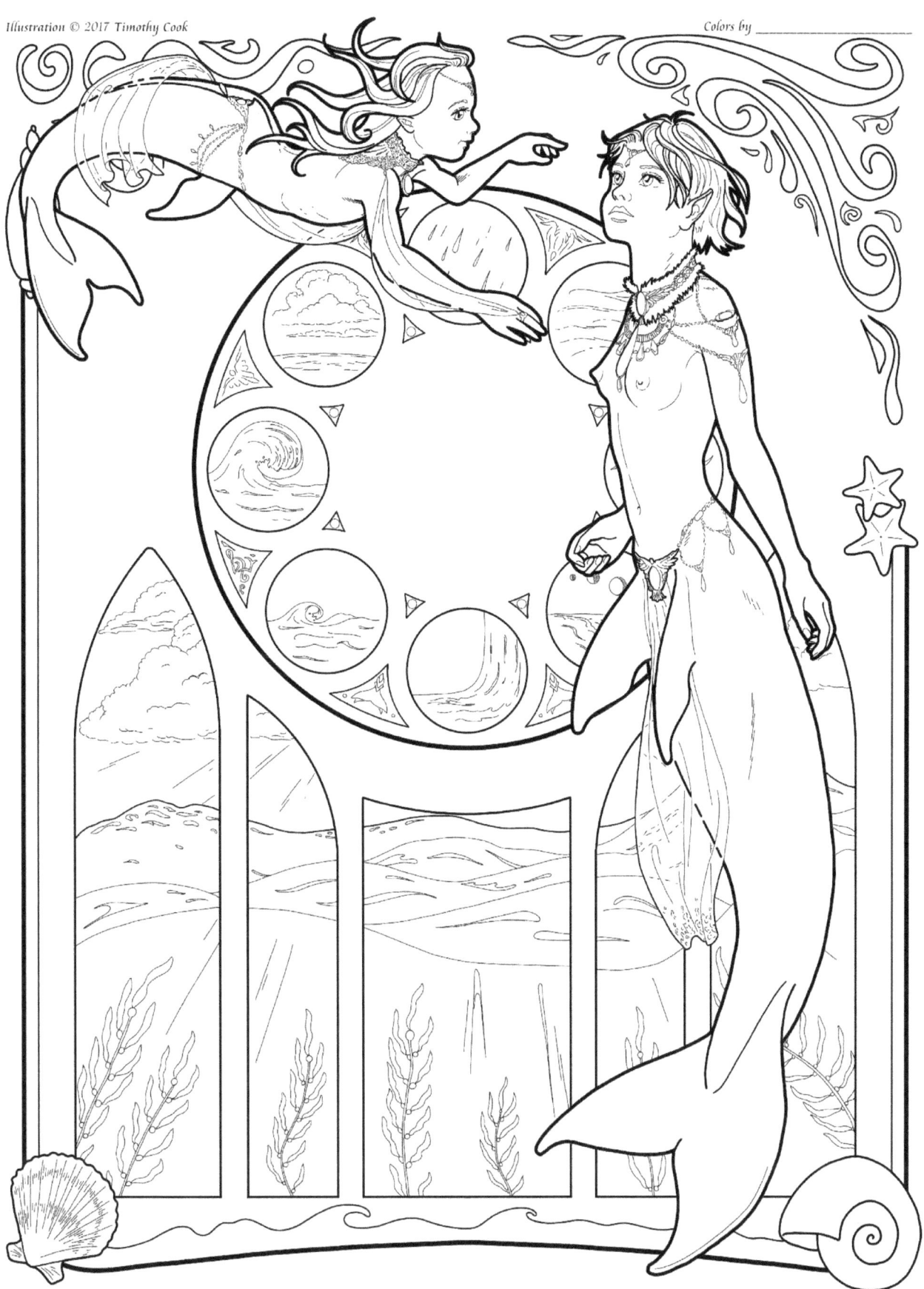

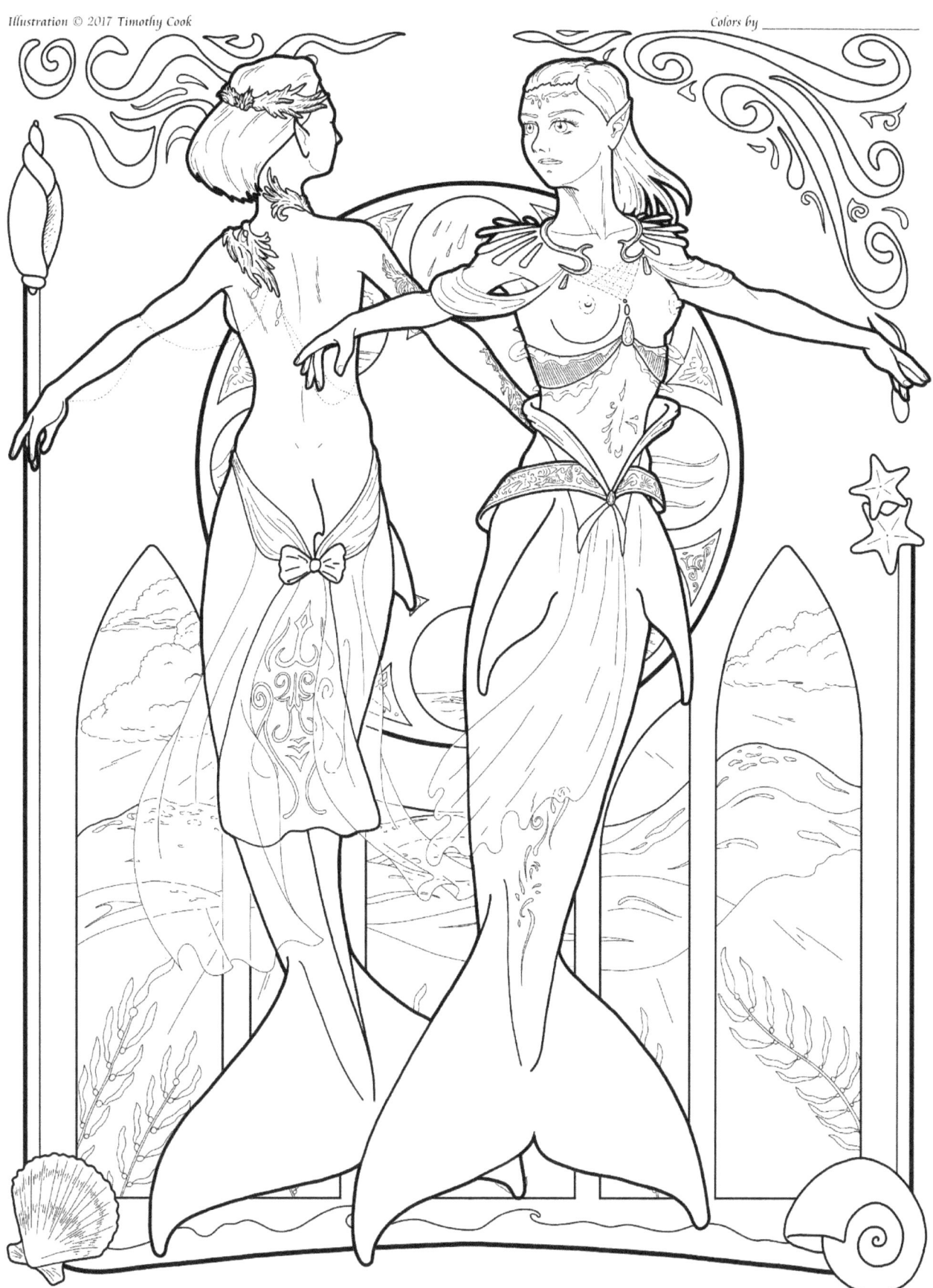

Colors by _____

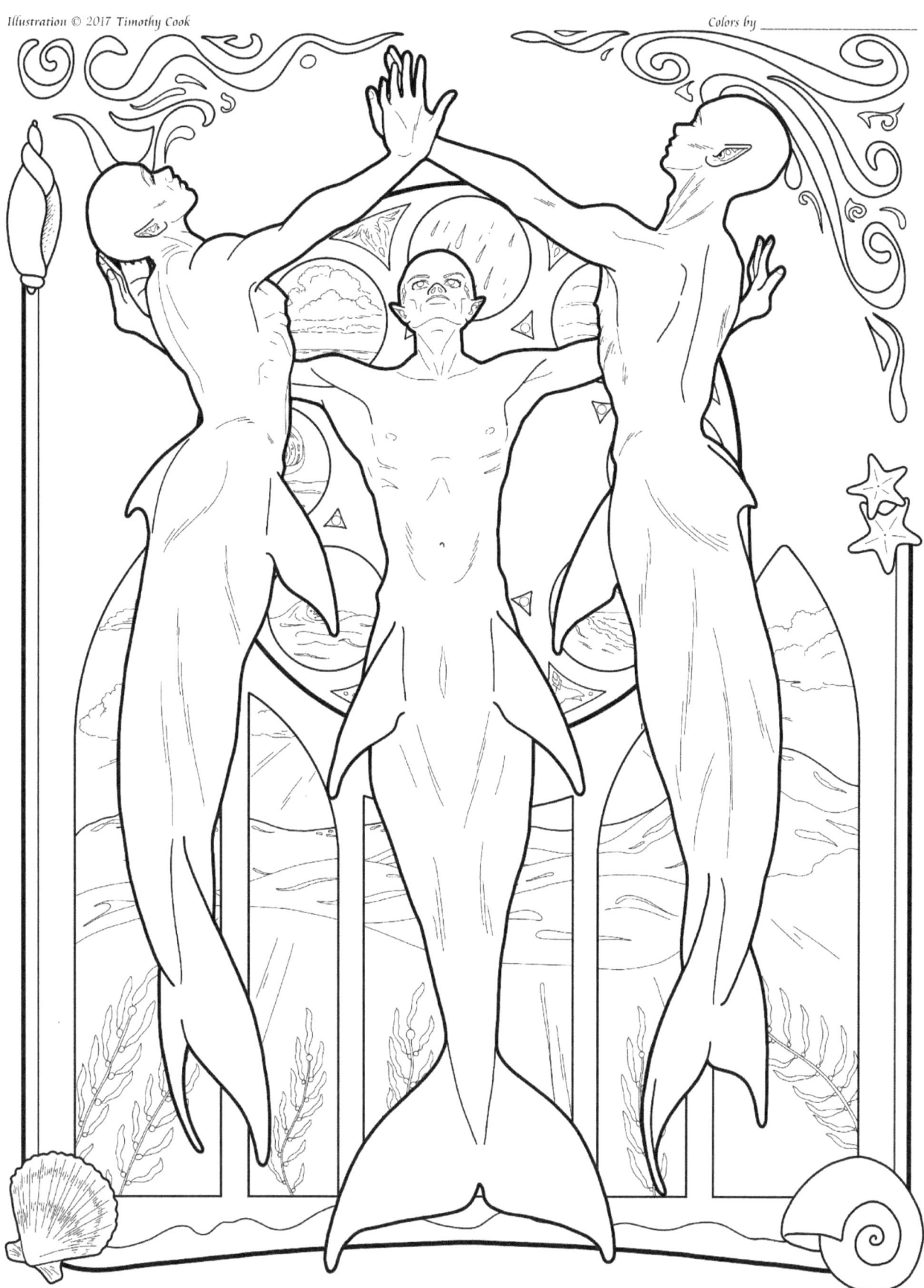

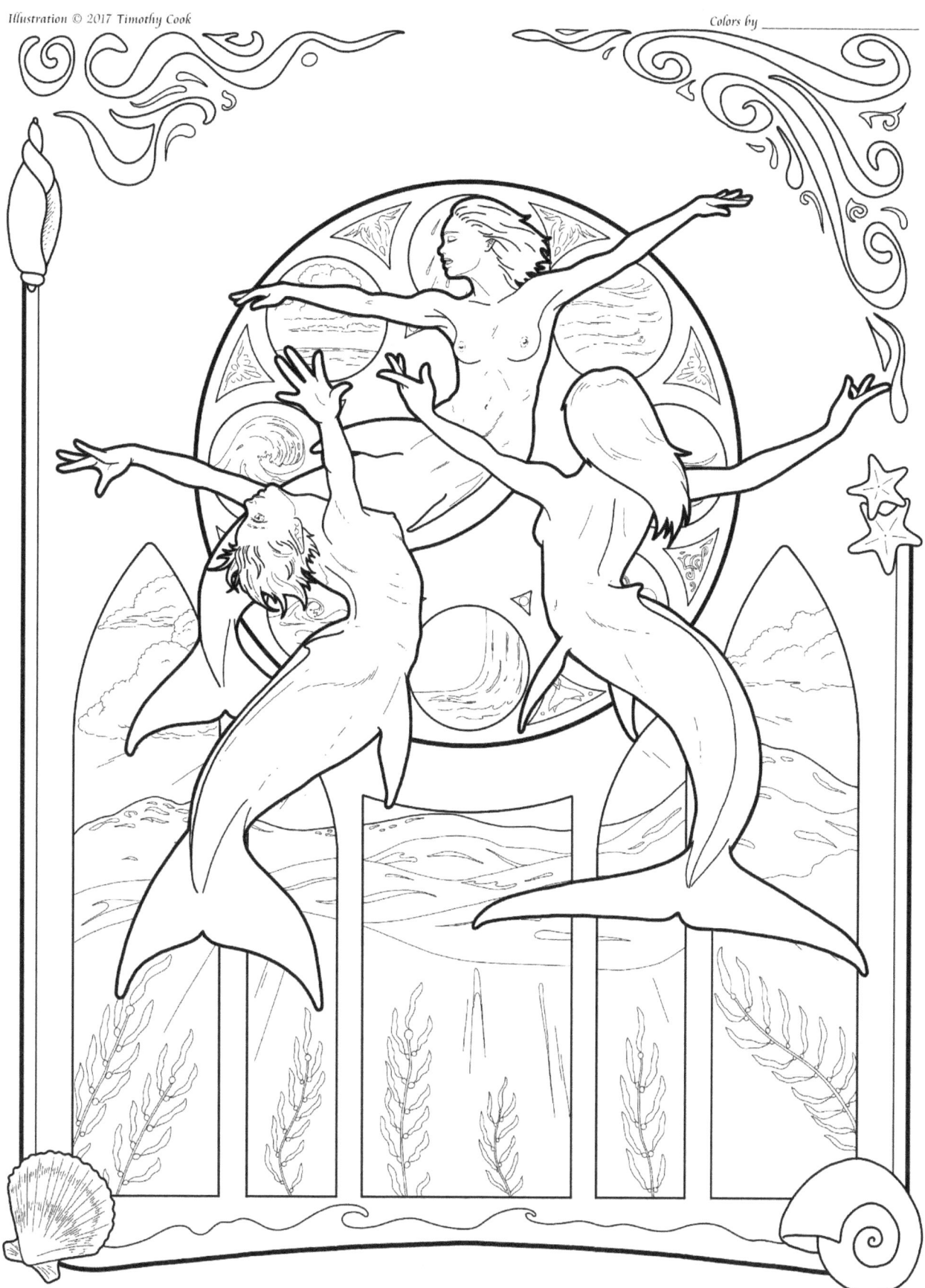

Colors by _____

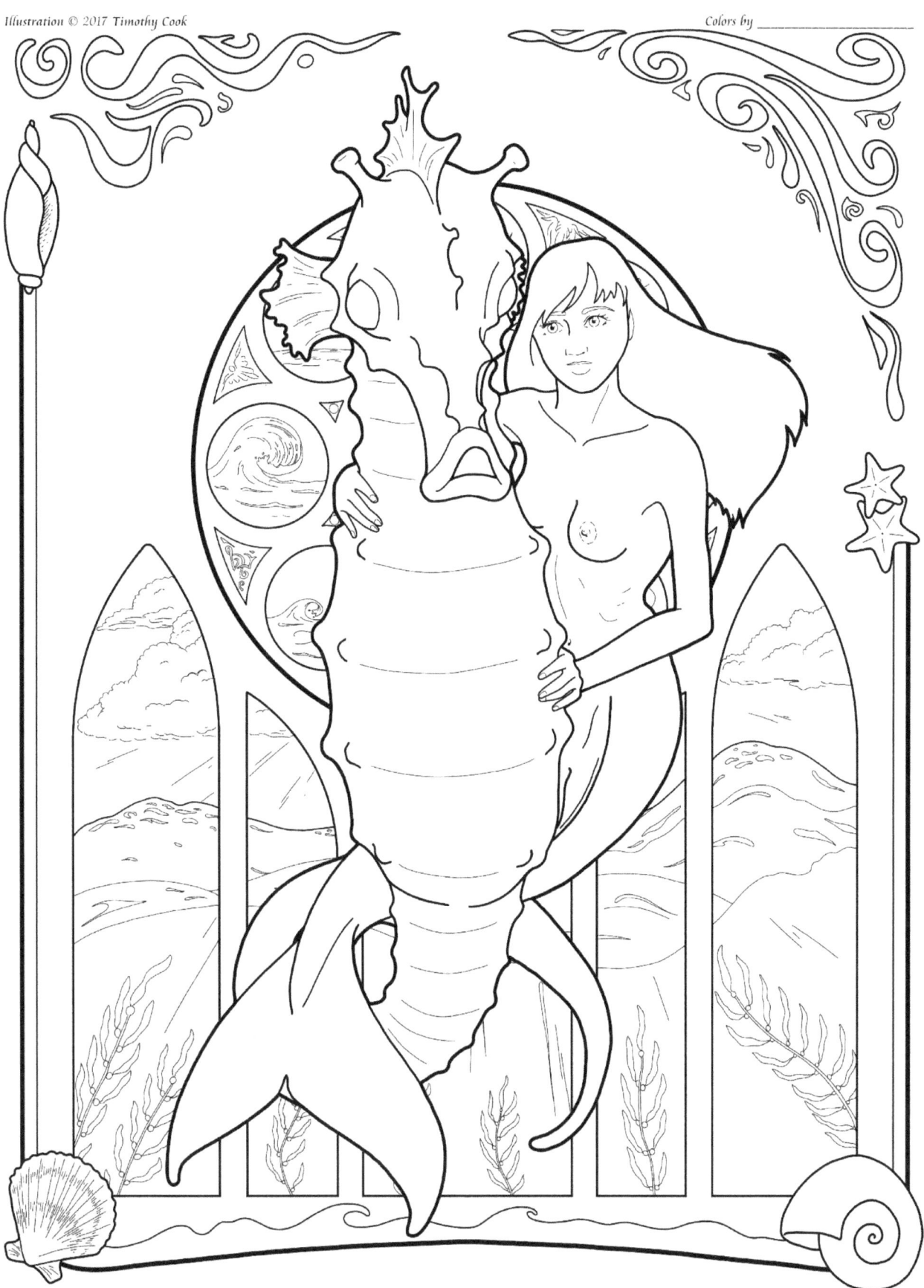

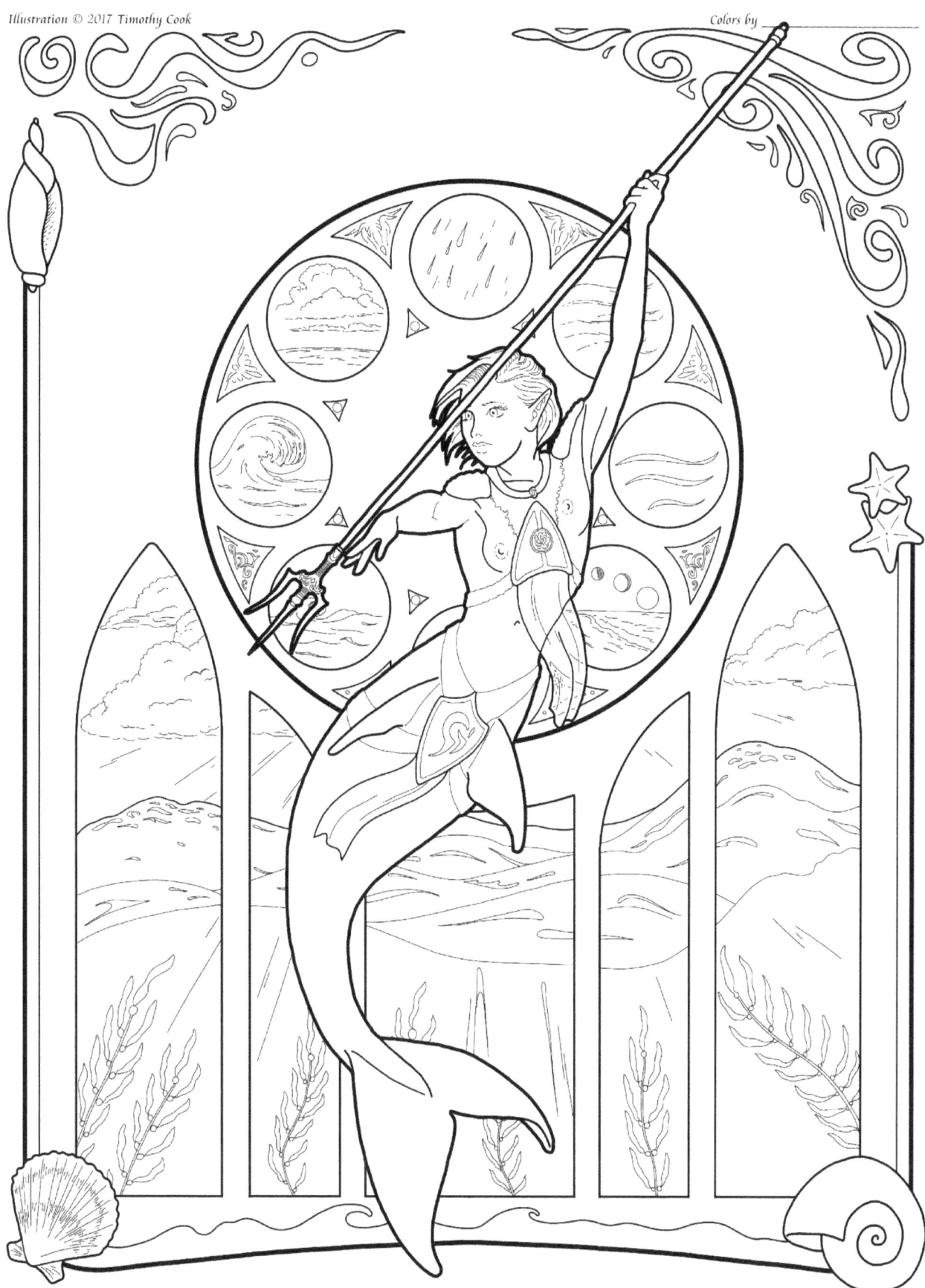

Colors by _____

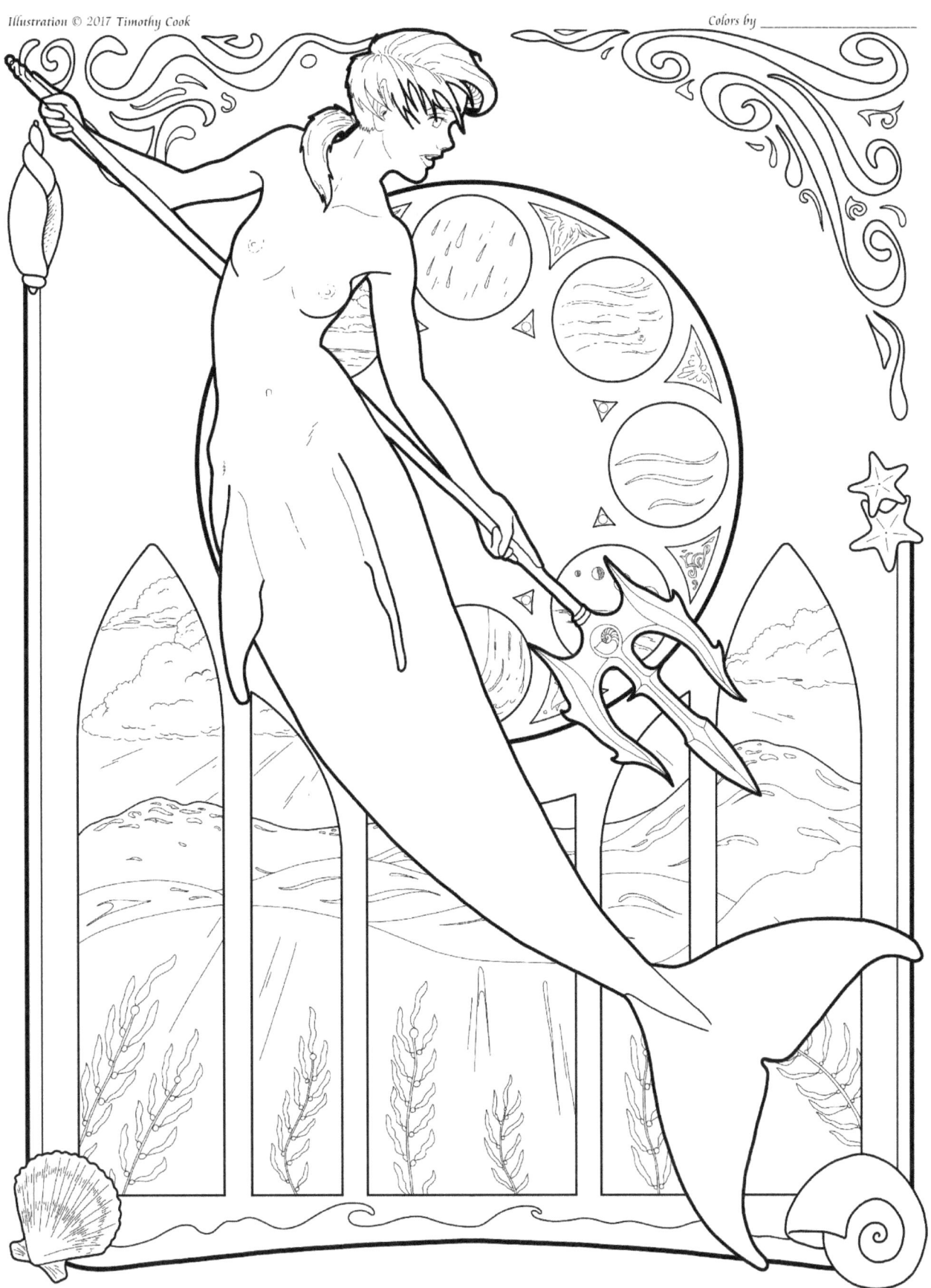

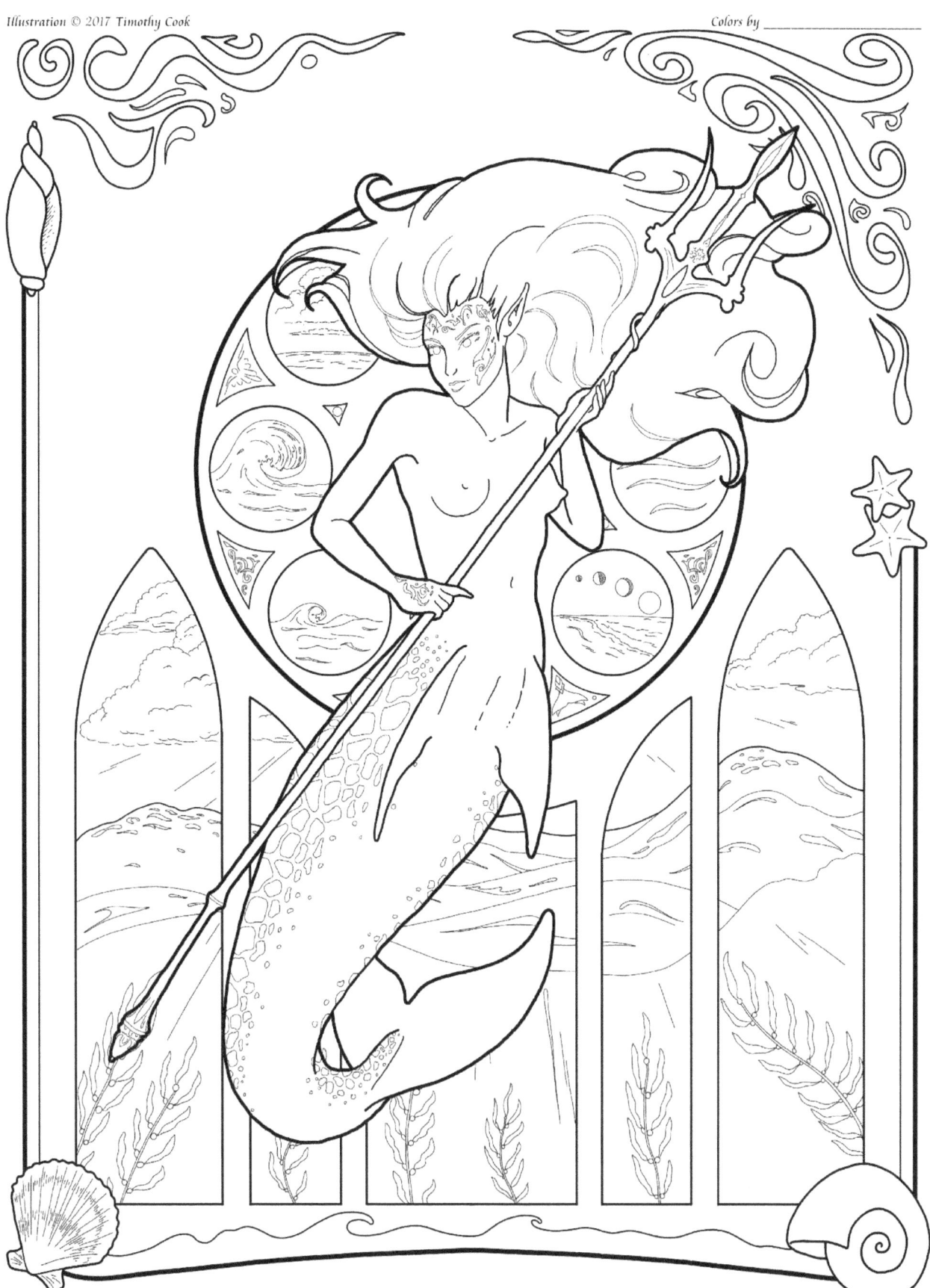